THE VICTORY OF CHRIST

Also by Dom Anscar Vonier
Published by Assumption Press

The Human Soul and its Relations with Other Spirits

The Personality of Christ

A Key to the Doctrine of the Eucharist

The Christian Mind

The Divine Motherhood

The Life of the World to Come

The Art of Christ: Retreat Conferences

The Angels

Death and Judgement

The New and Eternal Covenant

Christ the King of Glory

Christianus

The Spirit and the Bride

The People of God

Sketches and Studies in Theology

CHRISTOLOGICAL TRILOGY III

The Victory
of Christ

DOM ANSCAR VONIER

ASSUMPTION PRESS

2013

✠ Nihil Obstat.
Georgius D. Smith S.Th.M.,
Censor Deputatus.

✠ Imprimatur.
Joseph Butt,
Vicarius Generalis.

Westminster
July 9, 1934

This book was originally published in 1934
by Burns, Oates, and Washbourne.

Cover image: *Polyptych of the Resurrection*, Titian, 1520-22

Contents

Contents

FOREWORD

M UCH HAS BEEN WRITTEN BY THE DEFENDERS OF THE
Faith on the profound and far-reaching changes brought
about in the human race through the advent of Christianity. Again it
is a subject beloved of the apologists of Catholicism to show how the
Church has triumphed over and over again, and has come out victorious from the fiercest conflicts. In a more restricted field of observa-
tion hagiographers have been able to set forth the power of divine
grace in the hearts of individual men and women. The idea of a spiritual victory is the leading motive in such presentments of the history
of the Church; it is a victory that is observable and that can be made
the theme of any historiographer who has an eye for the great realities of the Christian faith.

The book which is now given to the public is not a work of apologetics but of theology. The victory of Christ of which it treats is
entirely a matter of faith; it is another aspect of redemption, and redemption is, of course, known only to faith. I have therefore chosen
the more difficult part, as theology is less accessible to the ordinary

mind than apologetics. I am encouraged, however, in selecting this difficult dogma by the thought that many a soul may be rendered happy by an increase of the knowledge of Christ's marvelous work and more courageous through an increase of the understanding of Christ's power over evil. To show the extent of that power is the main scope of this volume, and I am convinced that there is hardly a subject of Christian doctrine so appropriate to the needs of our day as the revealed truths concerning the defeat of the empire of darkness by Christ the King.

Anscar Vonier, O.S.B.,
Buckfast, Abbot.
Easter, 1934.

1

The Mystery of Christ's Glorification

THE VICTORY OF CHRIST IS AN INTEGRAL PART OF THE mystery of the glorification of Christ; it is that portion of it which has to do with the overcoming of obstacles. We ought therefore to begin by laying down the general principles that guide our faith in Christ's permanent exaltation.

The glorification of Jesus Christ is truly a mystery, that is to say, a truth and a fact greater than the mind of man can encompass. Like all other mysteries connected with the Incarnation it is incomprehensible both in itself and in its setting. The fact that One who not so long ago—nineteen centuries are a short period—walked on this earth, in all things resembling man, should now be in that state which is described as "sitting at the Right Hand of God" is, of course, beyond human comprehension, for the exaltation is an infinite reality, not a finite one.

Then the other aspect, the setting of the mystery, is in itself a problem that defies all human anticipation or parallel. The setting of the exaltation is the debased humanity from which Christ sprang, according to the flesh. It is true that Christ is raised above all names that are mentioned in this world or the next, but being exalted, He has not left humanity behind, He has not shed it, He has not cast it away, but He has retained all His connections with it. Humanity is truly the setting of the mystery of Christ's elevation as it is the setting, for example, of the Eucharist.

Now I say that this is a fact that baffles us, but which we have to accept as containing in itself no contradiction, that humanity should apparently remain so unelevated when its Head, Christ, is surrounded with infinite glory. This is, of course, no greater problem than the coexistence of God and evil, or the simultaneous realities of God's omnipotence and man's abuse of the free will which the Creator has given. Christianity is a series of such coexistences of diametrically opposite states, and we must accustom our minds not to think less well of the holy reality because the unholy one is by the side of it.

So Christ's glorification is for us the supreme reality which we see everywhere; it is not diminished through any denial of that splendor by the world; we know that Christ is in the glory of the Father. Our Lord's glorification is essentially to be conceived in terms of happiness for Himself. Through glorification He possesses in His humanity all that bliss which is due to Him in virtue of His being united hypostatically with Godhead. Whilst on earth much of that happiness was withheld from Christ's humanity—how much we have no means of knowing. Now, there is no possible check to the inundating gladness of the Divinity. He is as happy in His soul and body as is conceivably possible. Any sadness or pain now would be a contradiction of His state as the Son sitting at the Right Hand of the Father.

Christians here on earth may represent to themselves Christ as being a sufferer in soul and body. They may do this as a remembrance of all He endured during His earthly life. The sufferings of Christ may be said to haunt the mind of the Church, so vivid and so present is their memory. Christians may even think of Christ in the present as being the One whose Name is blasphemed and persecuted, whose love is unrepaid and forsaken. The sorrow for this ill-will on the part of the men with whom we live may inspire sentiments in the faithful towards Christ very near to sympathy as for one who is bruised and neglected. The mystical sense of the Catholic enables him to feel all those things as if Christ were suffering in him and he in Christ. But it is, of course, beyond all doubt that in Himself, in His self-subsisting personality at the Right Hand of the Almighty, Christ is infinitely far from the contact of evil, sadness and woe. He is truly the King of Glory and as such He rules the world with irresistible might, with a rod of iron, as the Scriptures love to put it.

Christ's glorification is the one article of the Creed that is to be held responsible for the Christian temperament. Our Christian outlook is what it is because we hold it as an obvious fact that our Lord and Chief is in the glory of the heavens. Such was the Apostolic mentality. The holy men whom the Son of God had chosen to be the foundations and the preachers of the new Kingdom went all over the world obsessed with the double vision of the abasement of Christ on the Cross and of the glory that followed:

> The ancients therefore that are among you, I beseech who am myself also an ancient and a witness of the sufferings of Christ, as also a partaker of that glory which is to be revealed in time to come (1 Pet 5:1).

They announced to the world One whom they conceived as filling heaven and earth with the splendor of His personality. Their distress was great that men could not behold Him whom they saw so clearly with the eyes of the spirit, that Jesus, whom God had exalted and who is the judge of the living and the dead. They suffered in their hearts for their newly-converted flocks, lest the dark horrors of persecution might obscure for them the vivid reality of the Christ in majesty. For to keep this faith alive is the main task of the Christian ministry. Glorification of Christ is the justification of the Christian religion, more even than that religion's inward merit and perfection. To give Christians confidence in their faith, through the greatness of the splendors of eternity, is the task of apostolic men of all times:

> You are of God, little children, and have overcome him (anti-Christ), because greater is he that is in you than he that is in the world (1 John 4:4).

Through our faith in Christ's glorification we are given the power to be superior to any might or glory that may try to raise itself up in this world against God.

St. Leo has an eloquent passage on this Christian mentality in one of his sermons on Christ's ascension:

> Whatever in our Redeemer was visible, passed into mysteries (through His ascension); and that faith might be nobler and firmer, sight was succeeded by doctrine, the authority of which might be followed by believing hearts, illuminated by rays from on high. This faith, increased by our Lord's ascension, and strengthened by the gift of the Holy Spirit, has not been over-awed by chains, nor imprisonments, nor banishments, nor famine, nor the sword, nor the teeth of wild beasts, nor punishments invented by the cruelty of persecutors. For this faith, throughout

the whole world, not only men, but even women, not only young boys, but even tender maidens, contended even to the shedding of their own blood. This faith has cast out demons, driven away sicknesses, raised the dead.

Hence also the blessed Apostles themselves, who, although confirmed by so many miracles, instructed by so many discourses, had yet been scared by the dreadfulness of the Lord's Passion, and had not received without hesitation the truth of His Resurrection, profited so greatly by the Lord's ascension, that whatever before had caused them to fear was turned into joy. For they had lifted up all the gaze of their soul to the Divinity of Him that was sitting at the Father's Right Hand; nor were they any longer hindered by the interposition of bodily vision from directing the glance of the mind to that which had neither, in descending, been absent from the Father, nor, in ascending, withdrawn from the disciples. Accordingly, then it was, dearly beloved, that the Son of Man, the Son of God, became known in a more transcendent and sacred way, when He betook Himself to the glory of the Father's Majesty, and in an ineffable manner began to be more present in His Divinity, when He became further off in His Humanity.

Christ's glory is immutable. It is now what it will be for all eternity: it acts now as it will act always. But not to all eyes is the glory manifested. To the spirits in heaven it has already noontide splendor; they see Christ exercising His power from one end of the universe to the other every hour of the present aeon. To the believer on earth, Christ is in the splendor of God, but neither with the eyes of the body nor of the mind can he see that effulgence. The infidel denies the glorification, and this denial makes him the infidel he is.

Christ, therefore, at the end of times will not receive greater glorification, but His glory will be manifested to all flesh. The great day of God is invariably spoken of as the manifestation of Christ's glory, as the unveiling of a wonder that existed and was present at all times, but was not seen by many. Not progress but manifestation is the difference between the state of Christ's glory to-day and that glory in the world to come. And what is true of Christ's glorification in general is true of Christ's victory, which is, as we have said, one portion of the belief that Christ sits at the Right Hand of God.

2

AN HISTORICAL SURVEY

IT IS CLEAR TO ALL THAT A VICTORY TRULY SO-CALLED MAY have a double perfection, that of quantity and that of quality. A victory of quality would only then be complete when every individual being who had been an opponent was brought into subjection by the victorious power. A victory of quality, on the other hand, would be so complete a conquest of all opposing forces that it might be truthfully said that all hostilities were over, that all the resources of the enemy had passed into the hands of the victor, that there was no chance of a reaction and that it would be a mere matter of time for the numerical results to appear.

Christ's victory has both these features, but not simultaneously. The victory of quality precedes the victory of numbers: the latter is delayed to a moment which is one of the Father's unrevealed secrets; the former is dated in a most precise fashion from the hour in which the Son of God rose from the dead; it is with us now, and will be with us forever, to be supplemented in due time by the second victory, that of numbers.

The Catholic mind is not indifferent to the numerical extent of Christ's achievement, but, in comparison with the qualitative intensity of the influence of Christ's work, numerical extent holds a secondary place. We are not directly interested in the question whether many are saved or few, but we are most keenly alive to the intrinsic power of Christ's salvation, to its virtue in removing all obstacles in the way of those who want to find God. Is there any kind of evil which Christ has left unconquered? or, if He has overcome it once, has the dark power a chance of rising again? It is precisely that unrestricted universality of victory that appeals to the Catholic mind and makes the universality of mere numbers to be a matter of less importance. If all men were saved by Christ in actual result, but were not saved in a supreme and irrevocable fashion from all evil, such salvation would be as nothing were it to be compared with the condition of those, many or few, who would be delivered from evil, *uberhaupt*, "at all," with no possible or imaginable limitation to their deliverance.

It is therefore in accordance with Christian sentiment to say that Christ would have labored in vain had He left one single enemy unchallenged and unconquered.

The older and more permanent Christian sentiment is concerned more directly, though not exclusively, with that absolute kind of triumph of Jesus which is the mystery of His resurrection. The earlier Christian period was the age when the fewness of the believers was not a scandal to the Christian mind. The opposition between faith and unbelief was an evident opposition between life and death, between light and darkness. This opposition, to the mind of the Christian, did not render light less light nor life less life. But even in those days of the clear ring of unchallenged redemption, the Catholic preacher was happy to point out the number of individual converts to the faith.

He loved to expatiate on the manifest power of the Gospel that carries everything before it. The two African preachers, Tertullian and Augustine, each in his day, gave vent to that legitimate feeling of Christian exultation. The older writer, Tertullian, in his *Apology*, is astonishingly aggressive at the thought of the numbers of Christians then alive:

> If we desired, indeed, to act the part of open enemies, not merely of secret avengers, would there be any lacking in strength, whether of numbers or resources? The Moors, the Marcomanni, the Parthians themselves, or any single people, however great, inhabiting a distinct territory, and confined within its own boundaries, does it surpass, forsooth, in numbers, one spread over all the world? We are but of yesterday, and we have filled every place among you—cities, islands, fortresses, towns, market-places, the very camp, tribes, companies, palace, senate, forum—we have left nothing to you but the temples of your gods. For what wars should we not be fit, not eager, even with uneven forces, we who so willingly yield ourselves to the sword, if in our religion it were not counted better to be slain than to slay? Without arms even, and raising no insurrectionary banner, but simply in enmity to you, we could carry on the contest with you by an ill-willed severance alone. For if such multitudes of men were to break away from you, and betake themselves to some remote corner of the world, why, the very loss of so many citizens, whatever sort they were, would cover the Empire with shame; nay, in the very forsaking, vengeance would be inflicted. Why, you would be so horror-struck at the solitude in which you would find yourselves at such an all-prevailing silence and that

stupor as of a dead world. You would have to seek subjects to govern. You would have more enemies than citizens remaining. For now it is the immense number of Christians which makes your enemies so few—almost all the inhabitants of your various cities being followers of Christ.

From the writings of St. Augustine one could cull a whole anthology of pregnant sayings concerning this same power of Christianity in the political world. One of the best known is found in his Enarratio:

> Pay attention at least to the glory of Christ's Cross. Already that Cross which His enemies insulted is marked on the forehead of kings. The world has proved the power. Christ "has overcome the world, not with iron but with wood": *Domuit orbem non ferro sed lingo* (St. Augustine, *Ennaratio*, in Ps 54).

On the whole the Christian ages have thought more of Christ's absolute triumph, with the result that their faith has suffered no scandal either from the sins of the believers or from the numerousness of unbelievers. The Middle Ages were certainly ages of faith through this very feature, the universal sense of Christ's supremacy. The external expressions of that sense are simply overpowering. They culminated in the position of the Papacy, in that unique phenomenon which ill will described as Papal imperialism, and which, if properly understood, is nothing else than the conviction shared by a whole civilization that all things are at the feet of the Son of God who reigns in heaven.

The period we call the Renaissance is a great assertion of the final victory of Christ in the plan of the universe, and this assertion is made by the Catholics and by the Protestants, though in different ways. Protestantism narrowed down the triumph of Christ to the redemptive mission of the Son of God and to the unshaken confidence on the part of man that Christ's supremely efficacious redemption was applied to individuals. Catholicism, on the other hand, went on, as it had done through the ages, giving a much wider interpretation to Christ's victory. The mind of Catholicism at that period is best expressed in the inscription which Pope Sixtus V caused to be cut on the ancient obelisk which by his order was placed in front of the Basilica of St. Peter, where it stands to-day:

> Christ is victorious, Christ reigns, Christ rules. May Christ defend His people from every ill. *Christus vincit, Christus regnat, Christus imperat, Christus ab omni malo plebem suam defendat.*

With all the losses which the Church had sustained through the Reformation movement there seems to be no diminution in the minds of Catholics in the unconquerable power of Christ. The Renaissance art has certainly done one thing magnificently, it has painted the triumph of Christ.

The question now arises whether we have kept that age-long sense of the triumph of Christ. It goes without saying that Catholics at least have never wavered in their faith; how could they, for Christ's triumph is an integral and indispensable portion of the Creed? The ancient Liturgy, which is exclusively a Liturgy of victory as we shall see by and by, is still in daily use without any modification; the hymns of triumph are on our lips whenever we join in the official prayers of the Church. This however would not prevent sentiment and imagination from being moulded differently, so that, in reality, with a theoretic faith that knows no shadow in Christ's glory, there may be much less of that exultation in the hearts of Christian men and women.

It would be difficult to analyze the causes of so vast a change of mentality. Weakening of faith would be the obvious formula in which to state the origin of the sad malady; but a diminished faith is again a result of other evil powers that are at work, not a cause that makes itself felt independently. The denial of Christ's position in the affairs of mankind is a comparatively recent phenomenon: we may assign to the eighteenth century the beginning of that hostile movement against the supremacy of the Redeemer. The whole of the nineteenth century has been the glorification of a civilization that boasts its independence of Christ, its complete self-sufficiency; in no wise will it acknowledge indebtedness to the Son of God for any of its achievements.

This almost universal self-sufficiency of the political world has become a grave temptation for believers themselves. So we see everywhere instances of the apologetic attitude of Christians, of the feeling of inferiority at least in sentiment and imagination which takes many forms, from the speculative to the devotional. We have become unduly worried by the conclusions of the so-called science of comparative religion. We make of the problem of the salvation of infidels an acute theological question, much to the damage of the doctrine of the salvation of the faithful through Christ. We admire too readily the works of the modern world, and we become unjust towards Christianity in our judgments of the Christian past. In politics we readily become the prey of catchwords and we are led astray gregariously like those who have not Christ for their Leader. Not infrequently our devotional life reveals a lamentable ignorance or forgetfulness of the essential doctrines of the supernatural order as it is in Christ.

The diminution of the spirit of worship in the world may be taken as the most evident sign of the decay of faith in Christ's supremacy. It is at the same time a cause and an effect. When men cease to praise Christ and to adore Him as their Lord and Master their feelings become more and more secularist, as, on the other hand, practical worldliness becomes increasingly impatient with all the duties of public and private worship.

3

THE FACT OF CHRIST'S VICTORY

THE TRADITIONAL CHRISTIAN CONCEPTION OF THE SON of God made Man is that of a Victor. This quality in Him is a special glory, clearly definable and distinguishable from all the other privileges that adorn the Person of Christ. It is not quite the same thing as being a Redeemer or a Savior, for both redemption and salvation might have been achieved without the specific element of victory. It is true that both redemption and salvation are very commonly spoken of as the victory of the Son of God, because in truth they were not brought about except through a great defeat of adverse powers, through a brilliant victory in the moral world. But this is not essential to the work of redeeming and saving. God might choose His elect, might save and redeem them, whilst leaving the hostile forces undisturbed in their position. But such has not been God's conduct through the mystery of His Son made Man. Not only are the elect chosen out of a world of evil, but that evil is overcome, is vanquished, so that it no longer has the air of a sovereign power.

It might be put like this: redemption and salvation are a purchasing of individual souls from the thralldom of sin, a sanctification of individual souls who were in a state of spiritual death: victory is a successful assault on evil itself, it is the dethroning of the king of the realm of darkness, it is a struggle followed by the discomfiture of an opposing and inimical power. The evil with which Christ had to deal was not only a disease, it was an enemy, one might say, a personal enemy. It would be an insufficient concept of the beneficent action of Jesus Christ here on earth to describe Him merely as a divine healer of both soul and body. He was a healer, indeed, of infinite efficiency, but the evil that met His eyes on all sides was more than bodily sores or spiritual diseases: He saw terrible, obstinate and resolute enmity pitted against Himself.

We may, of course, speak of the whole of Christ's activity as a victory, from His prayers to His charity in forgiving His enemies when expiring on the Cross. But this would not give to the term "victory" the technical significance it ought to possess when applied to the achievements of the Son of God. One is only a victor after a battle. Now Jesus Christ, besides His other great glories, has this renown, that He fought a great battle and that He remained the victor over a hostile force which was personal. Though we have to admit that the expression "victory" is largely metaphorical, it is none the less precise and exclusive in its meaning when applied to the Incarnate Son of God.

Another consideration is of importance here. The dethronement of the power of darkness could have been brought about by an act of God's omnipotence, just as, through omnipotence, all the elect could have been saved from a world of unconquered evil. Such a blow dealt by the arm of the Almighty would not have been a victory. It would have been the result of a divine *fiat*, as was the creation of light. For a victory, on the other hand, there must be a meeting of forces commensurate in some way, of created standards.

This truth is beautifully expressed by Pope St. Leo in his sermon on Christ's Nativity:

> For according to that fullness of time which the inscrutable depth of the Divine counsel ordained, the Son of God took on Him the nature of mankind in order to reconcile it to its Maker, that the devil, the inventor of death, might be conquered through that very nature which had been conquered by him. This conflict, undertaken for our sakes, was fought out with great and wonderful fairness of equality; inasmuch as the Almighty Lord does battle with that most cruel enemy not in His own Majesty, but in our lowliness, opposing him by the very same form and the very same nature, which shared indeed in our mortality, but was free from every kind of sin.

Christian thinkers of the higher order are always careful in assigning the reasons why it was desirable that the Son of God should be made Man, should be born in poverty, should be persecuted, should be put to death on an ignominious gibbet, in order to save mankind, though it is taken for an *a priori* certainty that innumerable other means were at God's disposal for the same purpose. The great doctors speak with awe of that "divine resolve," *divinum consilium*, that made God adopt the Cross as the instrument of salvation. St. Thomas Aquinas frankly professes that the real reasons of such a choice are "beyond the intellect of man" (St. Thomas Aquinas, *Summa Theologiae*, III, q. 1, a.2) It may be asserted, however, that the idea of victory is the richest and most satisfying concept applicable to this sublime matter.

The Son of God put forth, not His divinity but His humanity in the great struggle, so as to create an equality of condition between the combatants. Of whatever kind His enemies were, to the very last they were not certain of His being the King of Glory; in fact, as the ignominy of His death became the more evident, their conviction that He was not God grew stronger. The ignorance of what Christ was in His deeper self made it possible for His enemies to pursue Him to the end in the hope of exterminating Him from among the children of men:

> For if they had known it, they would never have crucified the Lord of glory (1 Cor 2:8).

It is certain that Christ's enemies had set out to destroy Him, to overcome Him. They wanted an evident sign that they were ultimately stronger than this mysterious and irritating personality. Crucifixion, if carried out to the full extent of its horrible possibilities, would be as loud a proclamation to the universe as human foresight could devise that, after all, the much-dreaded and mysterious man was nothing more than an ordinary mortal.

From the point of view of Christ's enemies the tragedy of Calvary was certainly a pitched battle, and death won the victory. To the very last they dreaded a reversal of fortune, some unexpected act on the part of the wonder-worker, which would make His persecutors the world's laughing-stock. But St. Paul's words just quoted seem to give a greater extent to that psychological state; the Apostle insinuates that the mightier minds of the evil spirits were also watching the results of the condemnation to death pronounced by Pilate. He speaks of the "princes of the world" (1 Cor 2:8) as being ignorant of Christ's true glory. This denomination, with St. Paul, is applicable to the unseen powers of darkness. That the Son of the Virgin was the object of determined hatred on the part of Satan from the moment He appeared in this world is revealed to us retrospectively by St. John in his apocalyptic vision:

> And there was another sign in heaven. And behold a great red dragon, having seven heads and ten horns and on his head seven diadems. And his tail drew the third part of the stars of heaven and cast them to the earth. And the dragon stood before the woman who was ready to be delivered: that, when she should be delivered, he might devour her son. And she brought forth a man child, who was to rule all nations with an iron rod. And her son was taken up to God and to his throne (Rev 12:3-5).

If the Son of Mary had been finally overcome by this array of hostility it would have been a defeat on His part. His enemies could have broken forth in shouts of triumph. But, on the other hand, if Christ emerged untouched in His Person from the death struggle, His enemies had to consider themselves hopelessly beaten. The word "victory" is the only true description of Christ's position.

The older Christian thinkers make of the circumstance that Jesus Christ's real nature was hidden from His enemies, human and discarnate, an inexhaustible subject of eloquent enlargements. They see in this terrible mistake made by man and Satan the true drama of Christ's fight. St. Leo has worked out the idea with astonishing fullness in his various sermons. The great Pope of the fifth century seems to take a positive delight in this aspect of Christ's death, which we might call the "surprise" aspect:

> And that He might loose mankind from the bonds of deadly transgression, He concealed from the devil's fury the power of

His own Majesty, and opposed him in the infirmity of our lowliness. For if the cruel and proud enemy could have known the plan of God's mercy, he would rather have set himself to soften the minds of the Jews into gentleness, than kindle them into unrighteous hatred; lest he should lose the dominion over all his captives, while attacking the freedom of One who owed him nought. So he was cheated by his own malice: he brought on the Son of God a punishment which was to be turned to the healing of all the sons of men. He shed righteous Blood, which was to be a ransom and a cup for the reconciliation of the world. What the Lord chose according to the purpose of His own will, that He took upon Him. He submitted Himself to the impious hands of infuriate men, who, while busy with their own wickedness, were doing the behest of the Redeemer (St. Leo, Sermon 62, *De Passione Domini*, "On the Lord's Passion", 40).

4

The Meaning of Christ's Victory

WE HAVE PROPOSED TWO POSSIBILITIES CONCERNING man's salvation from evil. The first is that God should elect His own from the midst of evil, without destroying evil, as such. The second hypothesis implies an act of divine omnipotence exterminating evil in all its forms at one blow. Neither of these possibilities did God choose, determining instead to save mankind through Christ, who destroyed evil, not by might, but by fighting against it as a hero. We can make a third suggestion which has to do with the work of Christ Himself. This suggestion is often made in Christian literature, and no one has put it more beautifully than St. Thomas Aquinas, who speaks thus of the redeeming Blood of the Son of God: "One single drop of that Blood can save the world from every kind of sin," *Cujus una stilla salvum facere totum mundum quit ab omni scelere* (Aquinas, *Adoro te devote*).

Christian theology, bearing in mind the supreme fact that the Redeemer is God, knows that the least human act on the part of Christ had value enough intrinsically to purchase man from the power of darkness, to overcome, in fact, all the world of iniquity. This assumption cannot be gainsaid. It was not necessary for the mere balancing of the ethical order that the Son of God should take upon Himself the great labors which He voluntarily undertook for our redemption. Nor would it be a satisfying statement to say that Christ did so much precisely with the intent that our redemption should be superabundant: that He added merit unto merit, suffering unto suffering, in order that there should be no possible scarcity of satisfaction given for sin. For we must remember that in very truth *una stilla*, "one drop" of His Blood, has inexhaustible power of propitiation for sin in all possible and imaginable emergencies. It has true infinitude of redeeming virtue, and nothing can be added to infinitude. We must then find another approach to the mystery of Christ's obedience "unto death, even to the death of the Cross" (Phil 2:8). We must think not only of the abundance of redemption but also of the glory of redemption; of the redemption that is a victory at the same time.

> To him that shall overcome, I will give to sit with me in my throne: as I also have overcome and am set down with my Father in His throne (Rev 3:21).

The work of redemption being by its very nature a victory, has for its principal result the exaltation of the Redeemer, an exaltation that implies the exaltation also of the elect, which is in itself redemption's first fruit.

Coming now to the actual relationship of effect and cause, it is, of course, impossible for man, without a special revelation from God, to know how the manner of Christ's birth, life and death overcame evil in all its aspects and was that supreme victory which makes of Jesus the Lord of heaven and earth. For we must take it for certain that there was in the mortal career of Christ and in His death that very force which brought low all His enemies and raised Him to the throne of God: "As I also have overcome and am set down with my Father in His throne." We may be made to understand how Jesus Christ through the manner of His life and death exercised the human virtues in the highest possible degree, how He practiced charity with incomprehensible perfection; but His behaving in so holy a way is not the explanation of His destruction of sin and Satan.

We have to admit another element, quite mysterious, that of God's free determination that certain definite acts of the Son of God made Man should be the death-blow to Satan's power. Without this divine determination the theology of redemption becomes well nigh meaningless. We forget too readily that the Son of God came for a work that embraces the whole created universe; St. Paul describes it thus:

> In the dispensation of the fullness of times, to reestablish all things in Christ, that are in heaven and on earth, in him (Eph 1:10).

Catholic theologians, following in this universal Christian sentiment, have always maintained that in God's wisdom the way in which the Son of God died was the direct and unerring road to victory. There was in that course a divine appropriateness for so great an end:

> The passion of Christ had a result which none of His previous merits had, not on account of greater charity, but on account of the nature of that deed, which was calculated to bring about such a result (III, q. 48, a. 1, ad 3).

The *genus operis*, "the special kind of deed done," is in the mind of St. Thomas Aquinas an indispensable factor in the work of Christ's spiritual conquest.

Christ is the instrument of God in this mighty work. Whatever He does or suffers is under the direct inspiration of the divine Spirit who moves Him for that very purpose. His human acts have an object far beyond their immediate moral excellency; they are the work which He came down from heaven to do, with a definite cosmic consequence that shakes heaven and earth. Through the Cross, Satan is conquered. Such is Christian faith; and it is a literal faith; that is to say, this physical reality, this stem of a tree cut from an olive grove, is to Satan more than the emblem of his defeat, it is the very weapon that defeated him, because God had so willed it. In order to understand the psychological mystery of Christ's terrific struggle, a knowledge of the psychology of the whole world of sanctity and sin is needed.

There is in Christ's history, as narrated by the New Testament writers, a visible element of victory, of which the fuller exposition is reserved to a later portion of this book. The very fact that the death of Christ was followed by the resurrection shows clearly that the Evangelists conceived Christ's career here on earth in the light of a victory as astounding as it was unexpected. This manifest and historic victory of the Son of God has been chronicled in a human way and it has the ordinary interests of human failure and success in the sense that we can follow the elements of this magnificent vicissitude of fortunes. This palpable form of Christ's victoriousness is, of course, an integral and very important part of the main mystery of the divine triumph. But when we say that Jesus Christ in the acts of His earthly career fought a battle and won a victory, we mean more than the things man saw and the "predestined witnesses" of the resurrection and the ascension beheld. Those very deeds of Jesus made Him victorious not only over His human enemies, but over His invisible enemies, over Satan and sin; it is as if on the Cross He had wrestled with sin personified in the prince of darkness.

It is with regard to this unseen conflict that we have to profess ignorance of all its phases. That there was such an assault on the army of evil by Christ is beyond all doubt, and the deeds of His mortal life were so many tactical moves in the battle. Christ not only merited the humbling of Satan, but He Himself, with His own valor, humbled the rebel spirit in the dust; Christ proved Himself to be the stronger of the two:

> When a strong man armed keepeth his court, those things are in peace which he possesseth. But if a stronger than he come upon him and overcome him, he will take away all his armor wherein he trusted and will distribute his spoils (Luke 11:21-22).

There was a battle in heaven between Michael and his followers on the one hand and Lucifer and his army on the other, at the dawn of the spirit world:

> And there was a great battle in heaven: Michael and his angels fought with the dragon, and the dragon fought and his angels. And they prevailed not: neither was their place found any more in heaven (Rev 12:7-8).

Nothing could be more remote from all our range of knowledge than the nature of such a war, spirit pitted against spirit. Still the reality of that decision of the sword of the spirit enters into the building up of our faith. We have to believe in the fall of the angels. Similarly, the contest between Christ and Satan through the Cross has no parallel in our experience: but this is no reason for doubting its historicity.

The whole procedure of that contest between Christ and evil is a true mystery, an event unfathomable for man. St. Leo again is eloquent on the recondite operations of the Savior:

> The Lord then was delivered up to the will of the infuriated enemies. In order to mock His Kingship He was compelled Himself to carry the instrument of His death, so that the vision of Isaiah might be fulfilled: "A child is born to us and a son is given to us and the government is upon his shoulder" (Isa 9:6). When therefore the Lord carried the wood of the cross, which He meant to change into the scepter of His power, He appeared to the eyes of the ungodly extremely debased, but to the believers a great mystery was rendered present. For this most glorious victor over Satan, this most potent conqueror of all adverse powers, carried the sign of His triumph as a brilliant ornament. He put on His own shoulders, armored as they were with insuperable patience, the emblem of salvation, which was to be adored by all nations (St. Leo, Sermon 59).

5

The Enemies

There are three hostile forces which Christian tradition considers to be the opponents of God: Satan, sin and death. Two of them are personal, Satan and sin, for by sin we must, of course, mean the sinner with his free act; death is an impersonal evil, yet it is justifiably classed as one of the three foes of God. For this we have Scriptural warrant: "And the enemy, death, shall be destroyed last" (1 Cor 15:26) says St. Paul, speaking of the general resurrection. St. John in the Apocalypse, describes death as an evil power that is finally cast into the place of reprobation. "And hell and death were cast into the pool of fire" (Rev 20:14).

It is not necessary for us to examine here the interdependence of those three evil realities. The very first page of our inspired Scriptures gives us sufficient insight into the close relationship between the manifestations of evil. Satan tempts man to sin and, the moment the rebellion against God is consummated, death becomes man's fate. Nothing more will happen on this earth in the matter of evil. The realm of evil was definitely established on the day of the Fall, through the triple tyranny of Satan, sin and death. Original sin makes all men to be radically children of wrath, and the actual sins of human beings, as they take place in the course of the centuries, are no new hideousness, but an imitation of the hideousness of the first sin. For the rebellion of Adam and Eve was the gravest sin ever committed by man: there can be no graver offence than the revolt of Adam against his Creator.

Human sin cannot be defined merely in terms of human influences; in every human sin there is the diabolical element, as it was in the first sin. Again, death is the work of Satan in a most direct manner. In proffering the great falsehood that disobedience could never mean death, but an illumination of the mind, the spirit of mendacity made of death the main object of his machination. He wanted man to fall into death:

> And the serpent said to the woman: No, you shall not die the death. For God doth know that in what day soever you shall eat thereof, your eyes shall be opened: and you shall be as Gods, knowing good and evil (Gen 3:4-5).

So Holy Writ makes the jealousy of Satan the origin of death. The Evil One was envious of man's immortality:

> For God created man incorruptible, and to the image of his own likeness he made him. But, by the envy of the devil, death came into the world (Wis 2:23-24).

It may seem strange to us who have so long been unaccustomed to look at God's plans in their entirety to hear it asserted that the main object in tempting man was to bring about his death. Yet it is not without deep significance that our Lord defines Satan as the arch-murderer:

You are of your father the devil: and the desires of your father you will do. He was a murderer from the beginning: and he stood not in the truth, because the truth is not in him. When he speaketh a lie, he speaketh of his own: for he is a liar and the father thereof (John 8:44).

Satan's lie brought about man's death, and death was the end he was set on. For although the interior sin of Adam was, for himself personally, a greater evil than the physical death that was to follow, from the point of view of Satan, if we may speak thus, death was the more important result, for it meant the destruction of a divine plan of immense greatness and beauty. Adam recovered interior grace himself through repentance, but death remains as a ruler; death reigned from Adam onwards, says St. Paul:

Death reigned from Adam unto Moses, even over them also who have not sinned, after the similitude of the transgression of Adam, who is a figure of him who was to come (Rom 5:14).

Every Catholic writer on these dread matters is, of course, conscious of a grave handicap: our contemporaries seem as incapable of taking an intellectual view of evil as they are unable to grasp the nature of goodness. They readily accuse theologians of giving to evil a look of majesty and power, when in reality it is nothing but an accidental frailty of human nature. Dogmatists, it is said, in order to create a *raison d'être* for the redemption, have first to invent the evil that would call for a redeemer. The ordinary human lapses, it is again said, could hardly be a justification for so stupendous an economy as is implied in the creed of the redemption.

Such easy superiority is much the vogue nowadays. But one moment's serious thought ought to be enough to make us pause in our light-hearted reading of mankind's conditions. It is evident, to begin with the obvious, that we are in contact with only a very small section of human life. What do we know of the ebb and flow of the well-nigh boundless ocean of human wills, as they are in truth before God? If our experience in our very limited sphere is not of the worst, what of the unplumbed depths of the vast multitudes of human beings who in reality are as far removed from us as if they had lived and died a thousand years ago? God's eye alone can see all that happens at every moment, in every heart. What do we know of the past—what of the future?

Then there is this problem of the corporate responsibility of mankind. Do we know the manner in which God looks at the men whom He has created? We ought certainly to be prepared for the assumption that to God mankind is a unity far beyond anything we can conceive. He sees in the last man that will be born on this planet the first man whom His hands created. The act of Adam is the act of all who are in Adam, the act of the human race which to God's eyes is a unit. The domination of Satan over that race is explained by the very first chapter of Genesis. For the order which God had created, for the order of innocence and immortality, Satan has succeeded in substituting the chaos of sin and death. The particular sins of all the children of Adam, which are all present to God's omniscience, are the result of that subversion of the original structure of grace and immortality.

Sin can be spoken of in the singular, as *peccatum* (sin), though its manifestations are more numerous than the drops of the ocean. It is always the original rebellion in one way or another, it is the stain upon our human family which is before God in its entirety as one moral factor:

> The next day, John saw Jesus coming to him; and he saith: Behold the Lamb of God. Behold him who taketh away the sin of the world (John 1:29).

The sin of the world constitutes, with Satan and death, the empire of evil. It is an active, organized and purposeful empire, because Satan dwells in sin and death. The three dark powers cannot be separated. To the end of history they appear in the same relationship in which they were first manifested, when Satan brought death into the world through the sin of the head of mankind.

6

THE DESTRUCTION OF SIN

THE MAIN DOCTRINES CONCERNING THE DESTRUCTION of sin by the word Incarnate are known to all Christians. This dogma is so vast that the simplest statement of it is the truest: we say, for instance, that God created the world, and these few words suffice for an adequate expression of the vastest of all facts: creation. We could not say more for this very reason, that all things without exception were made by God out of nothingness. So likewise we say that Christ destroyed sin, and we have said everything we can say. For truly Christ did it, and He alone did it, and He did it without leaving behind a single sin undestroyed. The greatness of that work makes its dogmatic expression easy, and Christians in their millions accept this immense fact in all literalness.

There can be no kind of transgression which has not been wiped away by the cleansing breath of Christ: from whatever angle we may consider sin, Christ's atoning power meets it. We may consider sin as an offence against the divine majesty, we may regard it as a disturbance of the moral order, we may look upon it as a slavedom of

Satan, we may View it as a stain on the human soul or as a guilt deserving eternal reprobation: every one of these aspects is met by the omnipotent grace of Christ's redemptive power. It is therefore a logical attitude amongst Christians to consider despair as the worst of all transgressions. By despair we mean the impression that may take hold of man that his sins are too great to be forgiven.

The subject of the destruction of sin by Christ is truly inexhaustible. Does not this doctrine fill our theological tomes? We believe in the remission of sin through Christ as we believe in the resurrection of all flesh, as we believe in eternal life; this remission is simply one of the basic facts of the supernatural world. My special object in this book is to bring home to the believer the implications of this great faith; to make him see what a victory Christ gained when He brought sin to naught.

In order to understand this more clearly let us remember that sin, in its very essence, is the exact opposite of charity; that it destroys radically man's friendship with God and renders him accordingly unfit for eternal life. Remission of sin then, if it is to be complete, must mean this—that man again becomes worthy of God, worthy of eternal life, worthy of everlasting abiding with God in the splendors of Beatific Vision.

Destruction of sin by Christ not only means a wiping away of guilt and stain, but it means a positive rebuilding of the broken spirit of man; man, through the redemption of Christ, is again made the temple of God. There is therefore in Christ's victory over sin more than a cleansing power, there is in it an infinite vivifying power, it is essentially a raising up of the countless multitudes of the spiritually dead.

Great as is the vision of Ezekiel, it is only a pale image of the supreme reality of the might of the Son of God to call out of their

spiritual tombs the souls buried in sin. The prophet beheld a lim-
itless plain covered with white bones, he despaired of ever seeing
those bones possessing life again; but what looked hopeless came to
pass through the breath of the Spirit "Which came into them, and
they lived: and they stood up upon their feet, an exceeding great
army" (Ezek 37:10).

Is it not a wonderful thought that every Christian may look
upon the Savior as being unceasingly in this very position of breath-
ing life into the innumerable dead of the world? He has destroyed
their sin, and He gives them life, and there is no end to that mystery
of life out of death. For we must bear in mind that this incomprehensibly great work has been done by this one Person—Jesus
Christ; there is no other agent, either principal or secondary, who
has concurred with Him. If ever a work was the work of one man
this destruction of sin is the work of the Man, Christ Jesus; to Him
the Father entrusted the work, to Him He left it to do, to Him He
set that task; Christ alone has trodden the wine-press of the world's
sinfulness and out of all nations there was not one with Him to help
Him.

This wonderful metaphor of treading the wine-press, as we know,
was at one time a very popular subject in Christian iconography; its
comprehension gave great credit to the generations that loved to
paint it and to gaze at it; they understood what we might call the exclusively personal factor in the work of the redemption; for although
we admit that it was in the power of God to destroy sin in many other
ways, Christian faith most persistently holds that all the sins of men
were put on the shoulders of the Incarnate Son of God and that He
bore them on the Cross. He truly appropriates unto Himself sin and
its effacement. It is therefore simply impossible to conceive of any

personality to whom the appellation "victorious" may be applied so truly as to the personality of Christ.

The reiterated expressions of the Scriptures that God put the sins of men on Christ, that God considered Christ as being covered with the sins of mankind, are extremely significative; they point to a great mystery of appropriation by Christ of this special work. In the theology of the Incarnation we are told that the Second Person of the Trinity was made Man with the exclusion of the First and Third Person; it is the Second Person who carried our sins and died on the Cross, and Christians go to their Lord as to the One who single-handed has achieved this great victory. Was there ever a conqueror like Him? Was there ever a courage like His? What power of darkness could remain where He shows Himself?

This atonement for sin in His own Person has given to Christ's humanity a new sanctity which is well described for us in matchless imagery by St. John in his apocalyptic vision:

> And his head and his hairs were white, as white wool and as snow. And his eyes were as a flame of fire: And his feet like unto fine brass, as in a burning furnace. And his voice as the sound of many waters (Rev 1:14-15).

This consciousness that Christ did the work of the cleansing of sin single-handed does not produce in the Christian mind a minimizing of each man's burdens or of each man's duty to make amend for his own sins; nor does it stand in the way of that very Catholic sentiment that Christians may be instrumental in atoning for each other's sins. It is quite in conformity with Catholic theology to speak of saintly men and women as being made victims for the sins of their brethren. Above all there is the role of the Virgin Mother at the foot of the Cross, entering more deeply into the mystery of the divine Victim than we can ever understand.

All such participations in Christ's propitiatory work are finite, and, of course, presuppose necessarily the supreme propitiation of Christ. With the Son of God we enter into the region of the absolutely infinite and into that sphere of atoning activity no creature, however holy, could follow Him. Whatever willingness and power there may be in Christians to work at the destruction of their own guilt is only a participation in Christ's all-sufficing and all-embracing satisfaction for sin. It is because the Son of God has destroyed sin so completely that we are able, each one in his own conscience, to repent for sin and to atone for sin.

In no other matter does Christianity show forth so clearly its unmatched superiority as in this, that liberation from sin is taken to be Christ's greatest gift to man. To keep alive amongst men a keen and practical appreciation of this liberation is the Church's greatest task, and in no other work does her unworldliness appear with such evidence.

Life has so many external servitudes which press on men and from which they desire to be set free; there are also the great political tyrannies of the world which may irritate and chafe the human mind to the last extremity; racial liberations are mankind's highest ideals and man is justified in giving his all and his very life to set his people free from the oppression of a tyrant. Today, as at all times, we assist at the working out of those irresistible idealisms which are a thirst for liberation. It is difficult for man, when thus carried forward on those waves of long-repressed enthusiasms for freedom from tyranny, to be made to feel that deliverance from sin is a most real deliverance, far exceeding in poignant interest any war of liberation known to history.

Nothing could give us a clearer insight into the spiritual excellency of Joseph, the husband of Mary, than this, that the angel described to him at once the greatness of Jesus in terms of spiritual liberation from sin:

> And she shall bring forth a son: and thou shalt call his name Jesus: for he shall save his people from their sins (Matt 1:21).

We can readily understand the radical difference between a society that has a practical belief in the doctrine of Christ's victory over sin and a society that, either through indifference or through materialistic infidelity, has no such belief. A deeper psychological gulf than the one brought about by these two mentalities can hardly be imagined. A people that considers it to be a historic fact, transcending all other events, that Christ has delivered it and is delivering it from its sins, has within itself a fount of perennial joy which no amount of material wealth can ever replace. Worship of that great Redeemer becomes naturally the primary task of such a people, and its power of suffering adversity in temporal matters is well-nigh inexhaustible.

7

THE VICTORY OVER DEATH

THE FACT THAT MEN DIE MUST BE CONSIDERED AS A most far-reaching thwarting of God's original plan. Death, in Catholic theology, is intimately associated with the original Fall and the sin that is inherited by all men. Man's rebellion in Paradise was a defiance of God, a demonstration that he would not die the death even if he disobeyed the divine command. So death has been considered by Holy Writ, not only as a punishment for sin, but also as an adversary of God's original plans.

We may indeed find it difficult to see how an event like death should be an enemy of God; but if we bear in mind, as already insinuated elsewhere, that death was the one purpose our arch-enemy had in view when he tempted man, we shall accept more readily the literalness of Scriptural language that makes of death an enemy. It is as if Satan, by bringing in death, had made an assault on the very city of God, and had obtained possession of one of its strongholds. So we find that Christ's resurrection from the dead is universally spoken of in Christian language as a victory over death. By this word "victory" Christian tradition means more than the simple fact that Christ, in His own Person, rose from the dead; it means that death itself was conquered, nay, was put to death, in the energetic language of the prophet:

O mors, ero mors tua, morsus tuus ero, inferne. O death, I will be thy death: O Hell, I will be thy bite (Hos 8:14).

It is unquestionably certain that God attached the restoration of His primitive order to the resurrection of the promised Messiah; the death which man's rebellion brought about was to be swept away by the event of Christ's resurrection. Here we may repeat what we say in other connections, that it would have been possible for God's omnipotence to heal this terrible disaster of death by a direct act of interference; but God chose another way, that the death of the One who by right was immortal, the Incarnate word of God, should be the end of death. So we may say that if Christ in His Person had not been able to conquer death, death would remain; but now He has destroyed it by showing in His own Person that death is not a permanent state, but only a passing condition.

We are justified, I think, in assuming that when Satan provoked man's rebellion and thus brought in death, the evil spirit thought that God's plans had miscarried finally; that death was a damage so great that it could not be repaired; that God Himself could not bring back to life that which was dead.

It is certain that Christ's bodily resurrection means infinitely more for the spiritual world than any other event except the event of liberation from sin; it means above all this, that God's power of making all things new, of restoring all things to their pristine perfection, is as great as His original power of creating all things out of nothing. The raising up of the dead is an entirely new manifestation of God's wisdom and omnipotence, more incomprehensible than the first creation of beings.

Now of this great divine deed of making all things to live, Christ Jesus is the hero, as He Himself has said: God is not only the God of the living but is also the God of the dead:

> And as concerning the dead that they rise again have you not read in the book of Moses, how in the bush God spoke to him, saying: I am the God of Abraham and the God of Isaac and the God of Jacob? He is not the God of the dead but of the living (Mark 22:26-27).

So we see Christ making of the resurrection a work which He came to do in the Name of His Father; He had received from His Father the command to lay down His life and to take it up again:

> Therefore doth the Father love me: because I lay down my life that I may take it again. No man taketh it away from me: but I lay it down of myself. And I have power to lay it down: and I have power to take it up again. This commandment have I received of my Father (John 10:17-18).

So likewise it is the will of the Father that sent Him that He should raise up the elect in the Last Day:

> Now this is the will of the Father who sent me: that of all that he hath given me, I should lose nothing: but should raise it up again in the last day. And this is the will of my Father that sent me: that everyone who seeth the Son and believeth in him may have life everlasting. And I will raise him up in the last day (John 6:39-40).

In Christ's resurrection there is the visible and the invisible result: the visible result is this: that His bodily resurrection is supreme and final evidence of His Godhead amongst men; the invisible result is precisely this, that death itself has been overcome in principle, a result that will be made manifest on the Last Day. In both senses Christ showed Himself supremely victorious. In our own days Christ's bodily resurrection is truly the world's great debate, because if it is proved that Christ rose on the third day Christianity is unassailable. Happily the world is full of excellent books showing forth the unconquerable validity of that testimony, Christ's bodily resurrection on the third day of His entombment.

We may confine ourselves here to one aspect of this great victory: no kind of glorification of Christ's soul would have been truly a victory; His body had to be alive again if His enemies were to be confounded. For like Satan of old in Paradise they had set their intent on death, that He whom they dreaded so much should no longer walk amongst men; that it should be proved that He was not God but only man through this very thing, death, for certainly if He were God He could not die. If He died, then He was not God. This was the reasoning of their jealousy; little did they care about His being a just man or a saint; they had no grudge against His soul, but they were determined to destroy His personality, His reputation; and death would do it most effectively. If the spirit only of Christ had been glorified, His enemies here on earth would have had every reason and justification to proclaim Him a mere man; but if He rose bodily from the dead, then all their worst fears were true; they had crucified God.

If it is objected that those very enemies of Christ were also the men who did not believe in His resurrection and that, consequently, they did not feel conquered by Christ, the answer is ready at hand.

Whatever impression the news that the dead Galilean had appeared again may have had on the minds of those men, one fact is clear, the resurrection of Jesus is an event of overpowering certainty for the believers of all times, and it is the believer who, in the first instance, is interested in the news of Christ's victorious rising. It is for him that this great testimony has been given. As for the unbeliever, he knows at least that faith in the resurrection of Christ is everywhere. It would be difficult for us to say what was the attitude of the persecutors of Jesus, of the men who put Him to death. No doubt we cannot be far wrong if we take it for granted that in their innermost hearts they admitted the fact of the resurrection. They did not become believers and worshippers in the supernatural sense of the word; they lived and died as Christ's enemies. Such contradictions inside the human conscience are quite possible; they died in their sin as Christ had foretold:

> Again therefore Jesus said to them: I go: and you shall seek me.
> And you shall die in your sin. Whither I go, you cannot come
> (John 8:21).

Resurrection from the dead is the one classical testimony of Christianity. All other testimonies are subsidiary to this main evidence. In the first centuries of Christendom the resurrection of Christ was almost exclusively appealed to by the preacher of the faith; the miracles that accompanied the ministry of the Apostles were signs that Christ had risen. The same economy of evidence holds good throughout the ages; whatever reasons for believing Christian apologists may adduce, they are only other ways of saying that Christ is risen from the dead and there is power in those who invoke the Name of the King of Glory. Christianity, we may say, is essentially resurrectionist; its first and its last appeal to man is this: Christ is risen from the dead. The empty tomb of Christ is the temple of Christian truth; a Christianity that was not resurrectionist would be as different from what we Catholics know it to be as a people of slaves differs from a victorious nation.

We come now to the mysterious power which Christ's resurrection possesses to conquer death in its widest meaning. Mankind is dead only provisionally; all men will rise again, will live again, and this in virtue of Christ's resurrection:

> Amen, amen, I say unto you, that the hour cometh, and now is, when the dead shall hear the voice of the Son of God: and they that hear shall live. For as the Father hath life in himself, so he hath given to the Son also to have life in himself. And he hath given him power to do judgement, because he is the Son of man. Wonder not at this: for the hour cometh, wherein all that are in the graves shall hear the voice of the Son of God. And they that have done good things shall come forth unto the resurrection of life: but they that have done evil unto the resurrection of judgement (John 5:25-29).

In strict theology we say that Christ's resurrection is the cause of the universal resurrection in a threefold fashion: it is a meritorious cause, it is an exemplary cause, and it is an efficient cause. Christ, through the charity of His death, merited His resurrection and in His resurrection He merited the raising up of all men from their graves. He is, too, the pattern of that tremendous transformation, the passage from death unto life; what was done in Him will be done in all men. But theologians say more: in all these matters we are dealing with God; the Son of God is risen from the dead in virtue of His own power; He is not raised up, He Himself, through the resources of His own personality, achieves that miracle; what He could do in Himself He can do with all flesh, all flesh has been given to Him in order that He should give life to it on the Last Day.

But the mighty circumstance that we are dealing with God in this matter of the resurrection also warns us and puts us on our guard lest we think that we have said everything. We only know the outlines of this great mystery. Even if we had no means of bringing home to our minds how Christ, through His resurrection, conquered death, we should still be full of enthusiasm for the great Victor. Christian tradition is so replete with the thought that on Easter Sunday death was conquered, that it would be egregious temerity not to attach to those utterances literal meaning.

8

THE TRIUMPH OVER SATAN

NOTHING IS MORE FAMILIAR TO CHRISTIAN THINKING than the defeat of Satan by Christ; on the other hand, few theological subjects are more difficult to explain. Scriptural language, patristic thought, liturgical formulas, combine in creating in our minds the impression that Christ met a formidable adversary, a personality of evil of immense power, and that He overcame that prince of darkness with finality. On the other hand, we find it difficult to put into exact theological language, first, the fact of that evil spirit's sovereignty, and then the nature of the defeat which he is supposed to have suffered at the hand of Christ. For Satan and his followers are creatures of God; they depend entirely on God for the breath of existence.

Their diversity from other creatures, from the good spirits for instance, is exclusively a diversity of will, not of nature. They are in opposition to God through a free choice of their wills; their natures are not altered; just as the essential nature of a bad man is not different from the essential nature of a good one. It is true that the fallen spirits have lost happiness, but this is only another way of saying that, through an act of will, they are in opposition to God. How then can it be said that Satan has power enough to be an adversary of Christ, when it is evident that by a single act of His will God could reduce the rebellious creature into the state of nothingness?

One of the explanations of Satan's sovereignty goes deep, and it is certainly to be considered as being an essential portion of Christian thought. Through sin, man became Satan's subject. It is one of the evil results of sin that it throws the sinner into the world of evil spirits, into the world of opposition. Through deliberate grave sin man abandons God, and this desertion does not remain neutral in its effects; positive hostile forces take hold of the derelict, through that hatred which Satan's perverted will exerts in every possible way. It would be very strange indeed if man, in opposition to God through an act of rebellion, could just remain where he chooses to remain, surrounded as he is with a world of active haters of God—the spirits of darkness—who are beings far superior to himself in power and in energy of hostility against God.

This appropriation of sinful man by Satan is certainly a readily comprehensible idea: "For by whom a man is overcome, of the same also is he the slave" (2 Pet 2:19). Another glimpse is given us in the book of the Apocalypse, where Satan is described as the accuser of man:

> And I heard a loud voice in heaven, saying: Now is come salvation and strength and the kingdom of our God and the power of his Christ: because the accuser of our brethren is cast forth, who accused them before our God day and night (Rev 11:10).

From words like these it is permissible to conclude that man's guilt gives a kind of juridical power; the power of the accuser, asking for punishment, not through a sense of justice, but from ill-will towards man. So it is said in theology that the sin of man gives Satan a right over man, that Satan's mastery is one of the punishments due to sin. We have, of course, to avoid anything that might have the appearance of juridical dealings between God and Satan, as if on a footing of equality. God owes nothing to Satan and the price of the redemption is not paid to Satan, but to God. But this much we may admit, and it will be sufficient to give a meaning to much of Christian language, that the reprobate spirit is clamoring for the exercise of God's justice, as he himself is condemned by that same justice. But when all that we can say with safety has been said, we have to grant that the words of the inspired books, as well as the current language of Christian antiquity and of ceremonial liturgy, point to a domination of mankind by Satan which is like the oppression of a human tyrant over his fellow-men. Christian language is realistic in the extreme, and so is Christian sentiment in the matter.

How, then, are we to visualize the breaking of that power by Christ? We can, of course, always say that our Lord merited for man, by His deeds of sanctity, the destruction of the empire of evil. But the whole tenor of inspired literature leads us to think of a more immediate, more personal combat between Christ and Satan, a conflict adumbrated by the temptation in the desert after the fast of forty days. The *vade retro, Satana*, "Get behind me, Satan" (Matt 16:23), that concluded that encounter was to be completed by a blow from the shoulder of such vehemence that Satan reeled and never rose again.

The personal power of our Lord over the demons in His public life, His irresistible influence against which they cried out, calling it a "torment," shows that there was more than a moral command: it was a true pressure of the advancing victor:

> And behold they cried out, saying: what have we to do with thee, Jesus, Son of God? Art thou come hither to torment us before the time (Matt 8:29)?

> And crying with a loud voice, he said: what have I to do with thee, Jesus, the Son of the Most High God? I adjure thee by God that thou torment me not (Mark 5:7).

> And when he saw Jesus, he fell down before him. And crying out with a loud voice, he said: what have I to do with thee, Jesus, Son of the Most High God? I beseech thee do not torment me (Luke 8:28).

It was a battle of the spirit, Christ's spirit being pitted against the proud mind of Satan. It was on the Cross that the main action was fought out, when Christ made Himself obedient to the extremity of an ignominious end. So Christian tradition has it that the prince of darkness knows of his complete discomfiture; he knows that his cause is irremediably lost. It is therefore the Christian's privilege to consider himself in every way stronger than Satan, to have no kind of fear in the presence of unseen enemies.

The contempt of the Saints for the devil is strangely at variance with the diffidence and the humility of those faithful servants of God. To make fun of Satan is one of the healthy manifestations of Catholic sentiment. It is only the unobservant who could not see the full meaning of that truly Catholic liberty to make the devil appear ridiculous. The terrors of somber spirits fill the unregenerate world; although actual devil worship may be confined to comparatively small sections of mankind, the worship of evil forces is widespread on the globe.

Christianity and Satan have become, through Christ's victory, an antithesis. The profession of Christ's faith and Satan exclude each other as day and night, not only in purpose but also in actual life. There is no kind of lien which the prince of darkness has over the Christian soul: he can neither hurt it nor seduce it. Through the virtue of our Baptism we enter into that very opposition which exists between Christ and Belial:

> But the things which the heathens sacrifice, they sacrifice to devils and not to God. And I would not that you should be made partakers with devils. You cannot drink the chalice of the Lord and the chalice of devils: you cannot be partakers of the table of the Lord and of the table of devils (1 Cor. 10:20-21).

There is a significant expression in St. Paul's epistle to the Romans: "And the God of peace crush Satan under your feet speedily" (Rom 16:20). The image of St. Michael with Satan under his feet is familiar to all of us, but St. Paul's bold words give us the right to emulate that angelic act of victoriousness. The Christian ought to stand, as does the Archangel, with the dragon under his feet. Such power, of course, comes to us from God; nevertheless, it is in us, it is we who are enabled to trample on the spirit of darkness; the Pauline phrase is certainly the last word in this matter of opposition between Christian grace and Satanic power.

So vast a subject was bound to figure largely in patristic thought. Thus we have endless allusions to this discomfiture of Satan in the writings and sermons of the Fathers. What I have already called the "surprise" aspect of the contest is the most frequent allusion in the voluminous literature of the defeat of the devil. St. Augustine is never more eloquent or more dramatic than when he is launched on this deep problem:

> It was necessary that Christ should come in hiddenness, so that He might be the object of a condemnation; but He will come with manifestation, so that He may condemn. For if He had come in the first instance with manifestation, who would have dared to condemn Him thus made manifest? Does not St. Paul say, "If they had known, they would never have crucified the Lord of Glory" (1 Cor 2:8)? But if He had not been killed, death would not have died.
>
> The devil was vanquished by His trophy. Satan rejoiced when through a deception he had succeeded in throwing the first man into death. By seducing the first man, he killed him: by killing the last man (Christ) he let the first escape from his snares. So the victory of our Lord Jesus Christ was celebrated when He rose from the dead and ascended into heaven.
>
> What you heard when the Apocalypse was being read has been accomplished, the Lion of the tribe of Judah has vanquished. He is called a lion who was killed as a lamb. He is a lion on account of His courage, a lamb because of His innocence; He is a lion because He is invincible, a lamb because He is meek. And the lamb that was killed overcame the lion who goes about seeking whom he may devour. For the devil is called a lion, not on account of his strength, but for reasons of his ferocity. For the Apostle St. Peter says, "you must watch against temptations, because your adversary, the devil, goes about seeking whom he might devour" (1 Pet 5:8).

And how does he go about? As a roaring lion, he says, seeking whom he might devour. Who would not fall into the jaws of that lion, if the Lion of the tribe of Judah had not overcome? You have the Lion against the lion, the Lamb against the wolf.

The devil exulted when Christ died and yet he was conquered through that very death of Christ. The devil thinking he had food had taken a bait. The sight of death rejoiced him, as if he were the overseer of death. But what was to him joy, became to him a trap. The trap of the devil is the Cross of Christ. The food he thought he had swallowed was the death of Christ. And behold, our Lord Jesus Christ is risen.

Where is the death that was suspended on the Cross? Where is the insult of the Jews? Where is the boasting and pride of those who shook their heads before the Cross, saying, If he be the Son of God, let him come down from the Cross? And He did more than they asked of Him in so opprobrious a fashion. For it is a greater deed to rise from the grave than to come down from the gibbet (St. Augustine, Sermon 263).

9

ANSWER TO THE MAIN OBJECTION

S O FAR WE HAVE NOT CONSIDERED ANY OF THE PRACTICAL difficulties which stand in the way of our whole-hearted acceptance of the doctrine of Christ's supreme victory. To the statement of and the answer to an objection which to many must seem formidable, we now turn our attention.

The objection is as simple as it is far-reaching. It is, in plain language, nothing else than this, that all appearances and all human experiences are against the totality of the triumph of Christ. In this matter we are confronted, not only by that sort of improbability which stands in the way of our accepting any of the mysteries of the Faith, but also by a seemingly direct contradiction between belief in an unchallenged spiritual overlordship and the realities that meet our eyes everywhere here on earth. With so much sin, with unbelief and infidelity everywhere in the majority, how could anyone not obsessed by a simplest optimism believe in the victory of Christ? Are we not deluding ourselves with mere assumptions, such as any religion might appropriate and claim as its own tenets? Christians, insinuates our detractor, will have to show a much larger measure of heroism than they have done or are doing, before the world will greet their Christ as a spiritual conqueror. Is it not much wiser for Christians to admit frankly the tragedy of their religion, the appalling chasm between the ideal and the real, and be satisfied to pay to their God a sort of cult of compassion for having disciples so immensely inferior to all He expects of them? Some of the less acrid of the scoffers at Christianity will even say that the religion of Jesus has a charm that is all its own, namely, an ideal God who suffers from the inferiority of His very un-ideal disciples.

Here we must remind the reader of the scope of this book. It is essentially and exclusively a work for the comfort of the believer. No one who does not hold the faith that the Son of God died on the Cross as a Victim of propitiation can have any part in the considerations here laid down. Anyone who accepts that initial article of faith has the capacity in him to understand the supremacy of Christ's victory over evil. We might say that to be admitted to the secrets of its results in the spiritual world is the recompense of so great a faith as is the belief in the redemption through the death of God.

As for the man who is either unwilling or incapable of sharing this great creed, it is evident that he cannot judge of human events except by human standards.

Now it is the proper characteristic of a propitiation for sin that is in the Blood of God Himself, that it atones for that very evil which is the scandal of many, the lack of correspondence on the part of man with the redeeming love of God. This evil, like all other evils, has been atoned for by the Son of God.

We may here mention a special instance of that resourcefulness of the propitiatory power of Christ which is always greater than any imaginable sin. The deicide of the Jews is the greatest sin committed by man since the Fall. It might seem to the superficial mind that it would have been almost better if God had not come down from heaven, so as not to expose man to the perpetration of a crime so intolerable. Such argument might be excused if it were not evident that in that very death of God of which men made themselves culpable there is found propitiation for the deicides themselves. It is only in the presupposition of an infinitely abundant propitiation for sin that we may believe in the effacing of iniquity, when iniquity is this very thing, the infliction of an ignominious death on a redeeming God.

It is, of course, evident that, with the Blood of God at its very source, as a redemptive and conquering power, Christianity has to adopt standards that are entirely different from human standards, and valuations for which there is no precedent in natural philosophical thought. The world's evils cannot be such any more in the same sense in which they would have been were there no such balancing power at the basis of the ethical universe as is the propitiation through the Blood of Christ. It may be difficult for us to understand how moral evil is less evil through this most sacrosanct presupposition. But that it is so is, of course, the very essence of the Christian faith in the Atonement.

Perhaps this is the most interesting and also the most baffling problem propounded to the human mind, to reconcile the guilt of sin with faith in the complete wiping away of sin by the Blood of Christ. In Christian doctrine, sin is atoned for by the Son of God long before it is committed by the free act of man, as Christ died to wipe away the sins of the future as well as the sins of the past. But in whatever way this great problem be solved, one thing is certain, the atoning act of Jesus is infinitely more important and weighty in the scale of moral values than all the possible sins of all men put together. This, of course, is an immediate and easily comprehensible consequence of the Incarnation, of the mystery of the God-Man. Anyone who holds that mystery is justified in believing in this immeasurable superiority of justice over sin, of atonement over offence; in one word, he has the right to live in the faith of the victory of the Son of God in spite of earthly appearances. He that has no such faith cannot lay claims to any such mental privilege; he cannot apply any other standards and measures than those of human ethics.

So we may lay it down as a principle that actual human sinfulness and present-day infidelity need not, in themselves, be signs that Christ's victory is not complete. Not one of those dark realities is beyond the redeeming and conquering power of the Son of God: He has made satisfaction for all of them.

We have no means of knowing what percentage of human beings actually profit in themselves by this divine victory, and will finally and eternally be saved. God has not made any confidence to man over this dread secret. But whatever be the ultimate percentage of lost and saved, one idea ought not to desert us, namely, that the numbers of the lost cannot in any way be regarded as a sign that the victory of Christ was less complete than it might have been; such calculations and appreciations are merely human ways of looking at God's work. We must hold it as the only rational attitude of mind that Christ's ultimate victory could not be greater. In whatever mysterious way the kingdom of the Son of God will be compensated for the loss of the reprobate, let us take it as an indisputable theological axiom that a complete compensation exists, so that the Son of God can truly say, "This is the will of the Father who sent me: that of all that he hath given me, I should lose nothing; but should raise it up again in the last day" (John 6:39).

To go through life with the kind of faith that is described in this book is no illuminism or unreasoning optimism. It is, on the contrary, the exercise of the finest gifts of the Spirit, the gifts of knowledge and understanding, which enable the Christian man to separate sentiment from truth, appearance from reality, eternal values from passing emotions. In another place we shall consider how ethical realism remains intact under a belief so intransigent in the nature of Christ's victory; and that it is possible to keep alive the horror of sin in a breast that glows with joy at the thought that all sins are atoned for by Christ.

It is always helpful to hear one of the great Christian thinkers in matters so contrary to human experience. Those fine intellects are proof against the disturbing influences of mere sentiment. St. Thomas Aquinas is famous for his unswerving adherence to the intellectual, and therefore true, value of Christian realities:

> Christ, through His passion, has liberated us from sins causally, in the sense that He has instituted the cause of our liberation, through which any kind of sin can be remitted, either past, present or future, as if a healer prepared a medicine to cure every kind of sickness, even a future sickness (III, q. 49, a. 1, ad 3).

> The charity of the suffering Christ was greater than the malice of those who crucified Him. Therefore greater was the power of Christ to atone by His passion, than was the power of sinning on the part of the crucifiers in killing Him. For the passion of Christ was not only sufficient, but superabundant to atone for the sins of those who nailed Him on the Cross (III, q. 18, a. 2, ad 2).

It would certainly have been in God's power to make the whole work of the Incarnation have this end, that all men should be preserved from all sin, as the Mother of God was preserved from all sin. But such has not been God's plan. The Incarnation is given for the purpose that all men should be redeemed from the sins committed by them. This work Christ has done, and He has not failed. That there should be those men who do not profit by the Incarnation in their own persons is not against the totality of the redemptive work, for no human being, endowed with free will, remains finally outside the grace of the Incarnation except through his own act.

There is a splendid doctrine of Catholic theology which brings out in a classical way the full meaning of Christ's victory over sin. An adult who is baptized is so completely liberated from all sin that between him and heaven there is no interval, so to speak, for were he to die directly after his baptism his soul would go straight to the Vision of God, whatever his previous life might have been. The sacrament of baptism gives him the full benefit of Christ's victory; he is in no need of any further purgation. Not to accept this doctrine would, in the words of St. Thomas Aquinas, "be an insult to the power of Christ's death" (III, q. 68, a. 5).

What we have already said of sin in this chapter is, of course, applicable to the power of Satan. The victory of Christ is as complete today as it will ever be; Satan's power is broken; and if the evil spirit is still active, his exertions are those of the leader of a broken and fast-retreating army. Satan is not chained up yet, as he will be at the end of times, using the apocalyptic language of St. John; he is still filled with a great anger and makes war on the saints, discomfited though he be. But we must simply admit that the evil spirits have not the least power over those who are Christ's and who are free from sin. The Fathers have tried to find popular formulas in order to express the condition of an enemy who is defeated but who is still active, full of evil resolve. St. Augustine's simple formula is as expressive as any other: "Satan can bark, but he cannot bite."

Christ's victory over death presents no practical difficulty. It is the dogmatic fact of the resurrection of all flesh. Let us remember that through the power of Christ's resurrection the human race in its entirety will be brought back to life irrespective of the ultimate fate of the elect or reprobate.

Once more we may emphasize the great dogmatic fact that the evils conquered by Christ are finite evils, whilst the victory is truly an infinite reality. It may not be easy for some minds to adjust themselves to such modes of thought, to see, for instance, how it is an infinitely better thing for us to be told that God by His Blood has redeemed the world than to be told that all men are saved. It ought not to be difficult, however, to realize that with God Himself at work everywhere human statistics of results would be very misleading measurements.

10

THE STANDARD OF VICTORY

THE VICTORY OF CHRIST IS A SUPERNATURAL REALITY which must deeply affect the thinking of Christians. If their Lord and Master is truly the triumphant King, Christians have a most efficient method of judging all things. There is simply no event, no kind of happening here on earth which does not appear insignificant by the side of this transcending reality, the victory of Christ.

The readiness to institute a comparison between the question of Christ's glory and human things is, for Christians, a most common way of enjoying their faith in the unseen glorification of the Crucified. It is not granted to the eye of the believer here on earth to behold the glory of the risen One, but once grace is accorded to every faithful soul, he can make that comparison between earthly things and the glorious Emmanuel. The Christian always knows that nothing really matters if Christ is risen, for that resurrection is victory without any limitations. If there is no such victory, then, of course, the Christian's lot is truly pitiable: "If in this life only we have hope in Christ, we are of all men most miserable" (1 Cor 15:19). So, on the contrary, if the splendid resurrection is an historic fact, then we have every justification in thinking little of this world and all its works, in thinking little of our own perils and tribulations.

The Christ who has conquered is so overpowering in His triumph that nothing can stand up against Him. We are powerful, as St. Paul was powerful, precisely through the answer of this conditional appeal: if Christ be not risen, what then? but if Christ be risen, what then? Why are we in danger every hour?

> I die daily, I protest by your glory, brethren, which I have in Christ Jesus our Lord. If (according to man) I fought with beasts at Ephesus, what doth it profit me, if the dead rise not again? Let us eat and drink, for tomorrow we shall die (1 Cor 15:30-32).

Life is simply inverted, it has an entirely different pole, according to the answer given to those conditional queries.

But Christ being risen, His sovereignty is unquestionable: "For he must reign, until he hath put all his enemies under his feet" (Gen 3:4-5). This is the usual procedure of the Christian mind; it is a faith of comparisons, it is a choice between two conditionals. If such a thing is true, then everything else falls into its place. What does it all matter, when we think of the glory that is in Christ? So in order to have the intellectual fruition of our faith in Christ's victory we are not under the necessity of beholding an actually submissive world, happy in the obedience of Christ. It is sufficient unto us to be profoundly convinced of the resurrection of Christ. From this we know that He rules the world with infallible security of justice and success.

In all matters, Christian faith is aprioristic. It is a greater, an immensely greater thing for us to accept the faith that Christ has redeemed mankind than to count the numbers of the saved. It is more important for us to know that from sunrise to sunset there is offered up a sacrifice of propitiation on the Eucharistic altars of the Church than to be able to diagnose the results of such a dispensation. Again, our faith in God's justice is our direct and infallible solution of any difficulty brought forward against the lot of the reprobate. Our knowledge of God's justice is the one thing that shapes our thinking, not sentiment concerning the possible state of the creature. The creature's state is very secondary and cannot possibly be in opposition to divine justice.

Another instance of the aprioristic nature of the Christian creed is the belief in prayer. We are certain that God has heard us, though we cannot demonstrably show it in pointing to results that are merely human. Such are the manners of the Christian faith right through, believing in a greater reality than the human factors, and establishing comparisons between the unseen and the seen:

> While we look not at the things which are seen, but at the things which are not seen. For the things which are seen are temporal: but the things which are not seen, are eternal (2 Cor 4:18).

So is it also with our faith in Christ's victory. A multitude of enemies making war on Christ here on earth in our days is a phenomenon which dwindles into nothingness by the side of the majesty of the victorious Christ. Our imagination may indeed feel impressed by the formidable array of hostile forces; but our reason, illumined by faith, sees all things in due proportion. To do this is faith's merit. The Christian to whom this habit of mind is foreign would be a pusillanimous believer. Not by believing in the wickedness of men but by believing in Christ's power to overcome all wickedness are we saved.

It is, of course, evident that in this matter [that] Christians identify themselves with a standard of thought that cannot be found elsewhere, and that can only be justified through the assumption of principles which are essential to Christianity in quite an exclusive fashion. In so many words, we think more of the power of God than of the state of the creature, because God's power is immutable and inexhaustible, whilst the creature is fallible and transient. By this we do not diminish the chance of the creature, nor do we reduce the creature's hopes, for we start with the assumption that God is more anxious for the creature's happiness than is the creature itself. The will of God to save man is infinitely earnest, whilst man has only feeble desires to escape from loss. So there is every justification for the aforesaid mental attitude.

We know that the counsel of God cannot fail, cannot be checked by any number of creatures abusing their freedom of choice. In this God shows Himself to be God, not only a demiurge. This mode of thinking, then, we also bring to bear on the victory of Christ. For us the whole issue is in this, as it was with St. Paul, did Christ rise from the dead or did He not rise from the dead? In other words, did Christ overcome all evil? If He did, all things are well, whatever the world may do in ages to come. It is, in a way of speaking, a greater announcement than if it were proclaimed that all men will be saved. For the victory of Christ is something greater than the corporate salvation of the human race. Christ's triumph means a conquest that goes far beyond even the highest interests of mankind, just as the mercies of God exceed by far all the occasions in which mercy may be needed.

11

CHRIST'S SUPERIORITY

IT IS NOT INFREQUENTLY MADE A REPROACH TO THE traditional Catholic Christology that there is an element of unreality in the Christ of official theology. The Jesus of the Gospels and also of Catholic piety is represented as having fought a tremendous moral battle in suffering and dying, when, on the other hand, it was absolutely clear to Him that the issue would be splendid beyond all earthly comprehension, and that no power in the world could either prevent or retard the triumph of His Person and of His cause. No earthly hero, it is said, was ever thus privileged; he had to plunge into the fray with no such assurances given to him. Would it not seem that the heroism of the earthly kind rings more true for that very absence of the clear and near vision of triumphant success?

We must indeed defend the doctrine of Christ's certainties against all comers, not only against the rationalists, but also against the well-meaning pietist. We must say that Christ would have not been more lovable, but less lovable if He had been less sure of His ultimate victory. An element of doubt, of fear, would have rendered Him less attractive to Christian contemplation. In other words, He would have been less of a hero. This, however, we must grant, that a marvellous and exceptional problem is found in Christ's certainties in the hour of His enemies and in the triumph of darkness: "This is your hour and the power of darkness" (Luke 22:53).

It is a spiritual phenomenon truly unique and it may be said without exaggeration that the whole mentality of Christianity is dependent on this very issue, whether or not Christ, in His abasement, had complete and unshakeable knowledge of the glories that were to come to Him. For if Jesus had such an assurance, it is evident that the evils that befell Him were essentially of a provisional character, that they were not powers to be dreaded, but trials to be undergone. Consequently, for Christians of all ages, it would be the only right attitude to meet the afflictions of the present times in the knowledge of a transient provision, not with the awe and terror that are inspired by an ultimate power.

Our Lord knew most certainly that nothing could finally hurt Him. He felt unassailable through all the laws and vitalities of His wonderful Personality: "For the prince of this world cometh: and in me he hath not anything" (John 14:30). There was in the Incarnate Son of God a perfect sense of proportion that made Him appraise the evils of the present life at their true valuation. If the term "philosopher" is justifiably applied to any one whom human evils do not mentally overpower, then Christ must be proclaimed to be the philosopher par excellence. Everything in Him made Him superior to that tyranny which human suffering and death exercise over the imagination of mankind, making those dreadful things appear as the true masters of human destiny.

But there was more in Christ than superiority of knowledge; there was in Him the power to conquer and overcome all those dark monsters. We must simply admit it as the only orthodox form of Christology, that Christ was in His Person, at all times, the uncontested master of death and all that is connected with death; physical evil and also human tyranny were powerless before Him whenever He chose to show forth His superiority.

The charm of that hero, Christ, is in this, that He submitted to those evils for the sake of the redeemed, in order to show that they could not really hurt what is essential in man. He took all human evils and death upon Himself with this very purpose, according to St. Paul, that death should lose for us its terrors, and that Satan, who tyrannized over man through the gloomy prospect of death, should be deprived of his most potent weapon, the apparent irrevocableness of death:

> Therefore because the children are partakers of flesh and blood, he also himself in like manner hath been partaker of the same: that through death, he might destroy him who had the empire of death, that is to say, the devil: and might deliver them who, through the fear of death, were all their lifetime subject to servitude (Heb 2:14-15).

So it is infinitely more consonant with the whole scheme of our liberation that Christ should have been, as Catholic theology has always represented Him, *inter mortuos liber*, "a free man among the dead," One who moved in the dark places of human existence with the light of divinity all round about Him, One that could not know sin, and if He tasted death, did so with the end that death should be swallowed up in the abundance of His own life. Thus Christ never speaks of His coming humiliation without mentioning the subsequent glorification; the resurrection on the third day is, one might almost say, a ritual formula with Him:

> Then Jesus took unto Him the twelve and said to them: Be-
> hold we go up to Jerusalem; and all things shall be accomplished
> which are written by the prophets concerning the Son of man.
> For He shall be delivered to the Gentiles and shall be mocked
> and scourged and spit upon. And after they have scourged him,
> they will put him to death. And the third day he shall rise again
> (Luke 18:31-33).

Any historian of Christ's life who does not give to this aspect of
the Gospels its true place, fails egregiously in his task. The insistence
of Christ on His complete immunity from sin and the tyranny of the
evil world, makes of His career something quite apart from all other
human histories. Not only does He leave it to the Christian of the
coming generation to find out how free He was, He Himself makes
use of every opportunity to proclaim this incontestable independence
of His, this power to bring low all that is against Him.

There is another aspect of Christ's passage here on earth which is
a kindred feature to the superiority just described. It is Christ's economy in the use of the powers that were in Him for the furtherance of
the Kingdom of God which He came to establish on earth. This is,
of course, a favorite theme with Christian preachers of all ages; and
the fact that this God Incarnate is a *locus communis,* "common topic,"
does not diminish the inexhaustible interest of the glorious subject.
Christ had His hour and Christ had His way for the work for which
He had been sent, and no power could deflect Him from His course
or induce Him to forestall His chosen moment:

> Now the Jews' feast of tabernacles was at hand. And his brethren
> said to him: Pass from hence and go into Judea, that thy dis-
> ciples also may see thy works which thou dost. For there is no

man that doth anything in secret, and he himself seeketh to be
known openly. If thou do these things, manifest thyself to the
world. For neither did his brethren believe in him. Then Jesus
said to them: My time is not yet come; but your time is always
ready. The world cannot hate you: but me it hateth, because I
give testimony of it, that the works thereof are evil. Go you up to
this festival day: but I go not up to this festival day, because my
time is not yet accomplished (John 7:2-8).

Is there truly anywhere a narrative like the Gospel narrative precisely from this point of view, the accumulation of testimonies that
the central hero has His fate in His own hands, that no one can
take His life from Him without His consent? This atmosphere in
which Christ moves has become, as I have said, the atmosphere of the
Christian mind; for the certainty that nothing can really hurt them
was meant to be the permanent medium in which all that adore the
Father are expected to have their being:

These things I have spoken to you, that in me you may have
peace. In the world you shall have distress. But have confidence.
I have overcome the world (John 16:33).

It was to be expected from Pope St. Leo that he would never give
any peace to his hearers on this very subject of Christ's freedom to
choose His own manner of life and death. The heresies of Nestorius
and Eutychius had disturbed the Christian conscience. For many it
had become an acute problem how to visualize the Christ-tragedy.
Was Jesus doomed to a terrible end without having a voice in the
matter, or would it not be wiser to attach no real meaning to the sufferings of the Son of God as they appear in the Gospels, the whole

event being merely an external show, as the Docetists would have it, who were akin to the Eutychians? The holy doctor reminds his Roman audience that Christ's infirmities are the fruit of Christ's power, as He willed to be weak from love to us:

> The two natures in Christ are but one Person, and there is only one Lord, the Son of God who, at the same time, is the Son of man; He took upon Himself the servile condition through a plan of love, without being subject to that condition through any law or necessity. For through an act of power He became lowly, through an act of power He became passible, through an act of power He became mortal. In order to destroy the sovereignty of sin and death He made the weak nature be capable of pain, without His strong nature losing any of its glory (St. Leo, Sermon 66).

It is no profanity to say that this is the sweet mystery of Christian humor, of that sense of the innate inferiority of all that tries to frighten man:

> And I say to you, my friends; Be not afraid of them who kill the body and after that have no more that they can do. But I will show you whom you shall fear: Fear ye him who, after he hath killed, hath power to cast into hell. Yea, I say to you: Fear him. Are not five sparrows sold for two farthings, and not one of them is forgotten before God? Yea, the very hairs of your head are all numbered. Fear not therefore: you are of more value than many sparrows (Luke 12:4).

The phrase "my friends" justifies our boldness in using here the word "humor." Christ is surrounded by a galaxy of men who can afford to make light of tribulation. Did not a smile play round His lips when He said of His disciples, big and strong men as they were, that it would take many sparrows to equal them in worth and weight?

12

CHRIST'S CERTAINTY

I N THE CHAPTER ON CHRIST'S SUPERIORITY WE HAVE already touched on the main principles of a most important topic in theology, the radical immunity of Christ from the powers of evil. In the present chapter we go one step further in the consideration of Christ's positive certainties concerning, not only His ultimate, but also His immediate triumph. It is taken for granted that the personality of Christ is essentially a mystery; Hypostatic Union can never be understood by man, nor can man estimate the consequences of that Union inside the personality of the God-Man. We cannot understand how our Lord possessed at the same time the glories of the Godhead and the infirmities of the Manhood; how He was omnipotent and weak; how He was impassible and passible.

Nestorianism, which divided Christ into two Persons, would apparently facilitate matters as, in the hypothesis of Nestorius, one could speak in Christ independently of Godhead and independently of Manhood, attributing to each its respective privileges and responsibilities. But the Catholic faith in the Oneness of Person in Christ makes such independent attributions heresies. The human in Christ has always to be considered in the light of the divine, and the death of Christ is not a merely human state, but the state of a divine Person.

Too frequently, I think, the analysis which devout writers pretend to undertake of what they call the "interior life of Christ," is tainted at bottom with crypto-Nestorianism; they readily read into Christ a life of thought and sentiment which is in reality the psychology of an independent human person, not of a human nature that is part of a divine Person. In no matter ought one to proceed with greater caution than in defining the activities of Christ's inward life.

We hold, moreover, that Christ's human mind, from the first moment of His conception, had the clear Vision of God, which it never lost. This circumstance alone would place Christ beyond all standards of human comparisons: no man knows what may be the workings of a created intellect when it is illumined through Beatific Vision. So we have at every turn this great fact, that Christ was absolutely certain of His future victory; the regularity of earthly seasons was to Him of less certainty, in a manner of speaking, than the advent of His triumphant glory. He knew with utmost clearness the price of the victory, and as for the actual coming of the day of glory for Himself, His mind had it present as a fact that was as good as accomplished.

So we have in our Lord's public utterances this constant reiteration of the certainty of His victory. Of doubt and hesitation concerning this all-important issue there is not a single vestige in the sacred Gospels. At no time does our Lord speak hesitatingly of His future, as if such hesitation were humility or meekness of heart; on the contrary, He glories publicly in the fact that no man has the power to hurt Him in any way.

This attitude of Christ's mind is identical with the vaster problem of His permanent consciousness that He was the Son of God;

a consciousness that did not come to Him gradually, but was in its noontide clarity from the very beginning of His human existence. It is noteworthy, however, that Christ more clearly and more frequently speaks of His triumph than of His Godhead. Catholic scholarship has had no difficulty in proving that Jesus Christ more than once said in clear words that He was the Son of God and therefore, God. It has become the fashion with the modernist to deny that Christ ever committed Himself to such statements, but even the modernist will not deny that Jesus of Nazareth most emphatically claimed a near triumph. In fact, as we know, this reiterated claim of the Gospels has been the occasion for many to accuse Christ of hyperbolical optimism. "Jesus," they say, "certainly declared that very soon He would be seen coming on the clouds of heaven, but generations of Christians have lived and died without seeing the promised spectacle."

Nothing is easier than to make a kind of description of Christ's attitude of mind with regard to this one thing, His near and absolute triumph. This victory, in a way, can be identified with the doctrine of the Kingdom of God, that Kingdom which is nigh when Christ speaks. The Kingdom is universally represented as being supreme, not only in its claims, but also in its efficacy. The work of the Kingdom may be a work of cleansing and purifying, but the cleansing and the purification are irresistible. Christ, the mighty Harvester, has the fan in His hands, to cleanse His barn; angels are sent out to separate wheat and cockle; the net that draws every kind of fish does not break, but the sorting of the fish, good and bad, is rapid and done as work is done, which it was always intended to accomplish.

Unholy elements, in Gospel thought, have no more power to stain or to retard the Kingdom of God than this world's impurities can hinder the progress of daylight. Now that Kingdom is to come at once, Christ's triumph is to come at once, nay, even the judgement is to come at once; all these expectations of Christ, all these magnificent promises need not wait for the last day of the world in order to have their fulfillment. The victory of the Cross, and the resurrection, with the advent of the Paraclete, fully justify Christ's declaration.

If we had to read all that Christ says concerning His victorious coming merely as so many prophecies of His return at the end of the world and nothing else, our lot as Christians would be hard indeed; there would be no ground under our feet; we might almost say there would be hope without faith, because we should not have the solid substance of our supernatural liberation invisibly surrounding us on all sides. It is indeed the exclusive genius of Christianity to possess this certainty. Whilst there is pressure and tribulation on all sides, whilst there is even the hour of darkness when the evil powers are let loose, there is in the midst of it all this reality of victory, not only the hope of a future reversal of conditions, but a present vision of the Kingdom of Glory, so that the martyr dies seeing Jesus standing at the Right Hand of God, as did Stephen, the first martyr; for this is ideal martyrdom, to behold the heavens opened, to gaze upon the triumphant Christ, even while a rain of stones crushes the life out of the body. Christianity has found it possible to reconcile adversity and prosperity, temptation and issue, persecution and exaltation in one and the same person, at one and the same moment. When the powers of darkness laid their hand on Jesus, that presumption of theirs recoiled on them as a thunderbolt of death. So is it with every power that lays its hand on the members of Jesus, persecuting Christ in His brethren.

Nothing is more significant than the emphasis of Christ on His approaching glorification at the very moment when He stood, like a criminal, before the High Priests:

And he said to them: If I shall tell you, you will not believe me.
And if I shall also ask you, you will not answer me, nor let me go.
But hereafter the Son of man shall be sitting on the right hand
of the power of God (Luke 22:67-69).

A greater immunity from the effects of human wickedness than the
one implied in these words of Christ cannot be imagined; yet such
is truly Christ's normal attitude during His life, and such is also the
normal attitude of Christ's Church to the end of times in the midst of
her enemies. There is truly no proportion between human adversity
and the glory that will be revealed in us. The exaltation which Christ
announces as awaiting Him without delay is out of all proportion to
the indignities He suffers in the courts of the High Priest.

It is one of our main Christian instincts to perceive this disproportion between human evil and the raising up of Christ through the power of God. It is mathematically true to say that the indignities which
Christ suffered in His Person are as nothing compared with the glories
that followed; moreover, that sitting of His at the Right Hand of the
Father is a position of such might and excellency that in very truth it
is as if all His enemies were His footstool. The vastest machinations
of Satan against Christ are, to the supreme Lord of Glory, an object of
derision. Nothing would be more contrary to Christian faith than the
mentality of which St. John speaks in the Revelation, when men are
overawed by the power of the dragon and the beast:

And all the earth was in admiration after the Beast. And they
adored the dragon which gave power to the beast, and they
adored the beast, saying: who is like to the beast? And who shall
be able to fight with him (Rev 13:3-4)?

A similar disproportion exists between those straitenings which are the normal condition of the Church, and her real glory, present and future. St. Paul asserts that there is no comparison between our present tribulation and the glory that will be revealed. We may extend further this apostolic method of appraising things. Between the real sanctity and power of the Church and the world's indifference and wickedness there is no comparison: one is a divine reality, the other is a negation. The people of God, the Church, has an immortality of duration which makes all other institutions appear ephemeral. Of that Kingdom it is said by the prophet that "it shall break in pieces and shall consume all other kingdoms, and itself shall stand for ever" (Dan, 2:4).

13

CHRIST'S GLORIFICATION THROUGH THE HOLY SPIRIT

THE EXTERNAL FORM OF CHRIST'S RESURRECTION IS THE last evidence of the resolve of the Son of God that here on earth, at His first coming, He would not show forth the majesty of the divinity that was in Him. To the eyes of the men who were privileged to behold the risen Christ, the external form of the Master was the same as it had been through life; even the momentary glorification of the transfiguration does not seem to have been repeated during the forty days which Christ spent on earth after His rising from the dead. The visions of glory and terror that belong to the Easter morning were not visions of Christ but apparitions of heavenly spirits; Christ Himself appeared invariably in the form to which the disciples were used.

This simplicity of behavior on the part of the risen Son of God is significative beyond words; the fact of His resurrection was the one thing that mattered and the time of external glorification had not yet arrived. For the purposes of Christian apologetics it is far more satisfying to see the figure of man only in the risen One, not the glory of divine majesty, because the complete identity of personality between the dead Christ and the risen Christ is of the highest importance.

If the risen Christ had appeared in the splendor of His glory that identity would have been less evident. That the resurrection made no difference whatever in the external appearance of Christ is truly a feature of divine artistry. There is peculiar beauty in the way in which St. Mark records the resurrection. For the Evangelist the supreme deed of the Son of God is as simple as the early rising of any man after a refreshing sleep:

> But he rising early the first day of the week, appeared first to Mary Magdalene, out of whom he had cast seven devils (Mark 16:9).

Could we not say that the manners of the great Victor in the hour of His triumph are truly divine?

The ascension of Christ into heaven, forty days after the resurrection, is Christ's last act here on earth, and in that act He does not break the self-imposed law of ordinary humanity. Though He is seen rising to heaven there seems, from the account given by the Evangelists, no reason why we should think of the ascending Savior as being suddenly glorified; so long as the gaze of His disciples followed Him, He kept the normal form of humanity:

> And it came to pass, whilst he blessed them, he departed from them and was carried up to heaven (Luke 24:51).

With Pentecost we enter into an entirely new sphere of divine manifestation. All those reticences and economies which give the Gospels their special characteristic disappear; there is no longer any question of not publishing the works of Christ, of not speaking of His transfiguration, of keeping silence over the wonders He had wrought;

on the contrary, publicity has become the key-note of the new deal-ings of God with man. The coming of the Holy Ghost on the fiftieth day after Christ's resurrection is the official proclamation by God Himself of the supreme victory of Christ. The descent of the Para-clete on that day ought to be considered by us, as it was considered by the Apostles, to be the external manifestation of the hidden victory of the risen Christ; the Holy Ghost is the herald of that victory; it is His mission to glorify Christ: "He shall glorify me because he shall receive of mine and shall show it unto you" (John 16:14).

That very special coming of the Holy Ghost, the Third Person of the Trinity, which took place on the first Pentecost is essentially connected with the great victory of Christ; the Spirit Himself, as He then appeared, is a Spirit of victory. The Incarnate Son of God, as we have seen, won the victory, but on this earth He never as-sumed the glories of that triumph. That triumph has become the office of the Third Person of the Trinity, the Holy Ghost, in that special manifestation, different from all the other advents of the Spirit, which we call Pentecost, and which, of course, is a permanent revelation.

The Paraclete is, to the end of times, the triumph of Christ personified in a divine Person, the Holy Ghost is amongst us in the Pentecostal sense as the external proclamation of all the hidden achievements of the divine hero, Jesus Christ. The Holy Ghost is so essentially a manifest presence that there is a kind of necessity for the Incarnate Son to withdraw His visible abiding:

> But I tell you the truth: it is expedient to you that I go. For if I go not, the Paraclete will not come to you: but if I go I will send him to you (John 16:7).

The Spirit of Pentecost has only one mission on the earth, to manifest in every possible way the glories of Christ, to convince the world that Christ has overcome all evil, that the prince of this world has already been judged by Christ. There will be no more silences, no more delays in trumpeting forth the truth, it will be unsparing, overpowering accusation and judging of the world for its refusal to believe in Christ. The sanctity of Christ, the merit and the justice of Christ will now be proclaimed to the ends of the world:

> And when he is come, he will convince the world of sin and of justice and of judgement. Of sin: because they believed not in me. And of justice: because I go to the Father: and you shall see me no longer. And of judgement: because the prince of this world is already judged (John 16:8-11).

Nor is there any longer a consideration for the infirmity of the human mind. Our Lord declared divine truth to the disciples gradually and carefully, as they were far from being ready for the intense light that was in the Master. Not so in the future; blazing light, without mitigation of its fierceness, will be the normal condition of God's dealings with man:

> I have yet many things to say to you: but you cannot bear them now. But when he, the Spirit of truth, is come, he will teach you all truth. For he shall not speak of himself: but what things soever he shall hear, he shall speak. And the things that are to come, he shall show you (John 16:12-13).

Truly the Spirit of Pentecost carries out in practice what Christ had announced:

Therefore fear them not. For nothing is covered that shall not be revealed: nor hid that shall not be known. That which I tell you in the dark, speak ye in the light: and that which you hear in the ear, preach ye upon the housetops (Matt 10:26-27).

Twice during His mortal life did the Spirit appear over Jesus, and in both instances He showed Himself as the glorifier of the Son of man. The two occasions are the well-known scenes of Christ's baptism in the Jordan and His transfiguration on the mountain. Both these scenes are, as we all know, entirely at variance with the general tenor of the Gospels, which are essentially the history of the hidden God:

And Jesus being baptized, forthwith came out of the water: And lo, the heavens were opened to him: and he saw the Spirit of God descending as a dove and coming upon him. And behold a voice from heaven, saying: This is my beloved Son, in whom I am well pleased (Matt 3:16-17).

This coming of the Spirit in splendor is an event that stands between two humiliations of the Son of God, His baptism at the hands of John and His fast and temptation in the wilderness.

In the transfiguration the Spirit appears as a bright cloud overshadowing Christ and His two companions:

And as he was yet speaking, behold a bright cloud overshadowed them. And lo, a voice out of the cloud, saying: This is my beloved Son in whom I am well pleased. Hear ye him (Matt 17:5).

Of this vision Jesus does not want a word to be spoken before the resurrection:

And as they came down from the mountain, Jesus charged them, saying: Tell the vision to no man till the Son of man be risen from the dead (Matt 17:5).

We may then give to the Spirit the name of Glorifier: as such He appears on two occasions in Christ's earthly career and as such He took possession of the Church and the world on the day of Pentecost. So the glory of our Lord here on earth is more than the remembrance by the believers of all He is and all He did: His glory is a divine Person; the Paraclete came to do this very thing which Christ had always shunned, to appear glorious. Nothing could be further from the intentions of God than that the Name of His Son should not be great among men. Only a few days before the beginning of the Passion Christ, whilst speaking to the people, was all at once seized with a great fear:

Now is my soul troubled. And what shall I say? Father, save me from this hour? But for this cause I came unto this hour. Father, glorify thy name. A voice therefore came from heaven: I have both glorified it and will glorify it again (John 12:27-28).

Glorification, then, is the dispensation of Pentecost, and truly the Holy Ghost is the herald of the victory of the Son of God here on earth; He announces to the ends of the world that Christ is risen and has conquered all things; that He sits at the Right Hand of God. St. Peter and the Apostles on the day of Pentecost and ever afterwards speak of the Spirit in this strain; He has come manifestly, He has come as the testimony of Christ's glorification. It is beyond doubt that the event which took place on the third hour of the day was of utmost publicity:

And when this was noised abroad, the multitude came together and were confounded in mind, because that every man heard them speak in his own tongue. ... And they were all astonished and wondered, saying one to another: what meaneth this (Acts 2:6, 12)?

Peter sees in all this the fulfillment of a promise; Christ was humbled, now He is glorified:

This Jesus hath God raised again, whereof all we are witnesses. Being exalted therefore by the right hand of God and having received of the Father the promise of the Holy Ghost, he hath poured forth this which you see and hear (Acts 2:32-33).

The life of the early Church is a transport of joy in the Holy Ghost. Christ's exaltation and the coming of the Holy Ghost are one and the same mystery, because the Holy Ghost is the Spirit of Christ sitting at the Right Hand of the Father. It is as if Christ Himself had appeared in majesty. The Spirit has all the power of the glorious Godhead.

As the Third Person of the Trinity has become the messenger of the Son of God in His exaltation, there can be no fear that Christ's glory will ever suffer any diminution in this world; there is a divine constancy in this work of showing forth who Christ really is. Neither men nor angels have been entrusted with this mighty message, the Spirit Himself is the Message; angels and men, as far as they are promoters of the name of Christ, are such, not through themselves, but through the Spirit that dwells in them. Sanctification of souls is only another word for glorification of the Son of God, for souls are holy in the measure in which they comprehend the greatness of the divine Victor over sin.

The language of our Lord concerning the work of the Paraclete is so precise and forcible that it is necessary to admit this very special glorification, besides admitting the more universal divine law that justice and truth must triumph in the end, and falsehood and iniquity, by their very nature, must sooner or later give way before the rights of truth and equity. Concerning the Son of God made Man there is more than this universal law of righteous retribution; there is direct exaltation as the counterpart of the humiliation: "For which cause, God hath also exalted him and given him a name which is above all names" (1 Phil 2:9). This magnificent recompense will only appear in its full splendor on the day when Christ will return in glory. In the meantime, however, the Spirit gives testimony that Christ is in the glory of the Father.

14

CHRIST'S VICTORY AND THE CHURCH

THE SPIRIT WHOM WE HAVE DESCRIBED AS THE HERALD of Christ's victory is Himself a mighty manifestation. He gives testimony of Christ by the assertion of His own presence on earth, and this assertion is made in an external, palpable fashion.

It is admitted that the Holy Ghost dwelt amongst men and inhabited the souls of the just at all times from Adam onwards, but not before the Pentecost described for us in the Acts of the Apostles had He manifested Himself in an external, visible manner for all men to see. In the baptism at the Jordan and in the transfiguration on the Mount the Spirit was indeed manifested visibly, but only to a few witnesses. So far His presence had been an invisible presence in the hearts of men; on Pentecost He manifested Himself visibly, so that in all literalness of language, St. Peter could say to the crowds that they had seen and heard the Spirit:

> Being exalted therefore by the right hand of God and having received of the Father the promise of the Holy Ghost, he hath poured forth this which you see and hear (Acts 2:33).

What happened on that third hour of the day was not primarily a mysterious inward transformation of man's mind, but an external sign to men that the Holy Ghost, who had been promised, had now arrived.

Right through the Acts of the Apostles we find that the coming of the Spirit, at Pentecost and later on, was to the early Christians as evident a truth as the coming of the Second Person of the Trinity—the Word—in the flesh. The Spirit took among the disciples the place which Jesus held when He was still walking with them; the Spirit was truly that "other Comforter" which Christ had promised:

> And I will ask the Father: and he shall give you another Paraclete, that he may abide with you for ever: The spirit of truth, whom the world cannot receive, because it seeth him not, nor knoweth him. But you shall know him; because he shall abide with you and be in you. I will not leave you orphans: I will come to you (John 14:16-18).

The Pentecostal marvel was not confined to the fiftieth day after Easter, for it was not a transient coming of the Holy Ghost but a true abiding; thus, for instance, when Cornelius and his household had received St. Peter's instruction the Holy Spirit fell on them:

> While Peter was yet speaking these words, the Holy Ghost fell on all them that heard the word. And the faithful of the circumcision, who came with Peter, were astonished for that the grace of the Holy Ghost was poured out upon the Gentiles also. For they heard them speaking with tongues, and magnifying God (Acts 10:44-46).

Peter was struck by the similarity of that event to his own experience in the Upper Room:

Then Peter answered: Can any man forbid water, that these should not be baptized, who have received the Holy Ghost, as well as we (Acts 10:47)?

He came back again to the similarity when asked to defend his conduct before the brethren in Jerusalem:

> And when I had begun to speak, the Holy Ghost fell upon them, as upon us also in the beginning. And I remembered the word of the Lord, how that he said: John indeed baptized with water, but you shall be baptized with the Holy Ghost. If then God gave them the same grace, as to us also who believed in the Lord Jesus Christ, who was I, that could withstand God (Acts 11:15-17)?

The coming of the Holy Ghost at Pentecost is in every respect as great a phenomenon in the divine economy of man's salvation as the Incarnation in the bosom of the Virgin. The mode of the coming of the Spirit is different from the way in which the Second Person of the Trinity came: the Son came assuming a human nature, the Holy Ghost came by giving evident signs of His arrival which no man could deny; but the coming and the abiding, in both instances, are equally real and lasting. The Spirit came, however, not so much for Himself as to give testimony of the coming of the Second Person, the word Incarnate. Christ had said this:

> But when he, the Spirit of truth, is come, he will teach you all truth. For he shall not speak of himself; but what things soever he shall hear, he shall speak. And the things that are to come he shall show you (John 16:13).

That the Spirit should not speak of Himself can only mean this, that His mission here on earth is complementary to Christ's mission, as the visible sign of Christ's invisible triumph; for in Christian theology Christ's triumph, as already said, is invisible, whilst the Spirit is visible. Christ will only appear at the end of times, but the Spirit has already appeared. Christ is received into heaven and will not be seen by the eye of man till the times be fulfilled:

> Whom heaven indeed must receive, until the times of the restitution of all things, which God hath spoken by the mouth of his holy prophets, from the beginning of the world (Acts 3:21).

But the Spirit comes out of heaven and men see and hear Him.

This visible mission of the Holy Ghost is, of course, of supreme importance in the whole of the Christian economy; if it were left out the Kingdom of God here on earth would be a mere idea, not a reality; the Holy Ghost, we may say, is the Kingdom of God, not in His invisible presence, I repeat it, but through what is manifest and visible. The interior graces and consolations of the Christian soul are a result of that external coming, and the presence of the Spirit is like a mighty voice proclaiming the fact that Christ is risen from the dead and sits at the Right Hand of God the Father in the glory of heaven.

The Catholic Church is the milieu in which the Holy Ghost carries out His mission of purification; the Church is essentially this, a people brought together by the Holy Ghost in the faith of Christ's victory. The first three thousand who were added "in that day" were won over because of what they saw and heard and from which they concluded that God had raised up "that Jesus whom they had crucified." The same work goes on over the whole world through the Church to the end of time. It is only a glorified and victorious Christ that could win adherence: not one who led a holy life and became the innocent victim of His enemies, without power over His own destiny.

The Catholic Church then, must at all times be viewed in the light of Christ's victory; it is her very life to believe in that victory, to feed on it, to glorify it through the Spirit that is in her. Any diminution of her faith in Christ's victory would be a death-blow to her; for she is not living on an edifying memory, but she fights for the King of Glory whom the heavens have received.

This faith in Christ's victory is truly the continuation of Pentecost; it is as great a marvel as the signs by which the Spirit manifested Himself. The purpose of the Spirit was thus, in the language of St. Peter, to show forth the great fact that God had glorified His Son. As long as there are men united in that same faith the work of the Spirit knows no abatement. He does what He did at Pentecost. He shows His presence because through Him we believe that Christ is risen and glorified.

The Catholic Church shows forth in every act of her life something of Christ's victory; her faith, her prayers, her sacraments, her combats, her whole organization, proclaim that her Head is the One who has overcome all evil and has acquired eternal glory. In order to be a Church of victory she need not be without assaults from the outside nor without blemishes in her own children. But one thing is essential to her, she must be able to meet every outside adversary and she must be able to cleanse away every sin that is found in the heart of any of her members; and this the Church has always done, and for this reason we are more than justified in proclaiming her the Church militant, which can only mean the victorious Church.

It is not without deep significance that the mystery of the resurrection, the mystery of the Spirit and the mystery of the forgiveness of sins are shown as united in the sacred Gospels. When Christ comes back from the dead, when He shows Himself to the Apostles, He breathes on them the Spirit and gives them power to remit sins, for the exercise of that power is truly the complete Christian Easter:

> And when he had said this, he showed them his hands and his side. The disciples therefore were glad, when they saw the Lord. He said therefore to them again: Peace be to you. As the Father hath sent me, I also send you. When he had said this, he breathed on them; and he said to them: Receive ye the Holy Ghost. Whose sins you shall forgive, they are forgiven them: and whose sins you shall retain, they are retained (John 20:20-23).

The power of forgiving sin in the Church is the one great trophy which Christ brought back to His Apostles when He returned from His triumphant battle; He did not bring the grace of complete sinlessness for the Church here below, but He brought the greater grace of the remission of sins in His Name, because He had conquered sin. It is as if Christ, in that moment of supreme happiness, was overpowered Himself by what He had achieved on the Cross and in the tomb and in Limbo, the complete conquest of sin, and so His first words to His disciples are to be these: "whose sins you shall forgive, they are forgiven." They are truly the words of a conqueror. Christ had forgiven sin in His own lifetime, but now He makes a gift of that power to His Church to the end of times, without any reservation.

It is perhaps the unfortunate result of our being familiarized with divine utterances that makes it difficult for us to see the transcending glory of a Gospel passage like this. Had it been left to us to find out which were the first words of Christ to His disciples at so astonishing a moment would it have occurred to us to put remission of sins in the first rank? But happily we are not asked to speak for God; the Gospels are essentially the dealings of a divine Person and therefore dealings which are mostly unexpected and incomprehensible. Still, does it not sound as if Christ, with infinite graciousness, told His Apostles: "Here I am once more, and since we parted I have done what I set out to do: I have destroyed sin. Therefore go forth and forgive sin wherever there is sin to be forgiven."

We may conclude this chapter with an extract from St. Leo's sixty-third sermon. More than anyone else this profound and illuminated thinker seems to have possessed the capacity of perceiving the supernatural reality in its entirety, without being side-tracked by the transient phenomena of human weakness:

> So then, all those things which the Son of God both did and taught for the reconciliation of the world, we do not simply know of by the history of past events, but feel even now by the power of the present operations. He it is who, having been brought forth by the Holy Spirit from a Virgin Mother, by the same inspiration makes fruitful His undefiled Church, so that through the Baptismal childbearing is produced an innumerable multitude of children of God, of whom it is said, "who were born, not of blood, nor of the will of the flesh, nor of the will of man, but of God" (John 1:13).
>
> He it is in whom the seed of Abraham is blessed by the adoption of the whole world to sonship, and the patriarch becomes the father of nations, while the promised sons are born, not carnally, but by faith. He it is who, making no exception of any nation,

forms out of every people under heaven one flock of holy sheep, and daily performs what He had promised in the words, "And other sheep I have, which are not of this fold; them also I must bring, and they shall hear my voice, and there shall be one fold and one Shepherd" (John 10:16). For although it is to blessed Peter chiefly that He says, "Feed my sheep," yet it is by the one Lord that care is taken for all the shepherds themselves, and those who come to the Rock He nourishes in such pleasant and well-watered pastures, that numberless sheep, strengthened with the fatness of love, hesitate not themselves to die for the Name of the Shepherd, even as the Good Shepherd was pleased to lay down His life for the sheep.

He it is in whose suffering not only the glorious courage of Martyrs has a share, but also the faith of all who are new-born in their actual regeneration. For while they renounce the devil, and believe in God; while they pass from the old life into the new; while the image of the earthly man is laid aside, and the form of the Heavenly is put on; there takes place a certain appearance of death, and a certain likeness of resurrection; so that he who is put on by Christ and puts on Christ is not the same after the laver as he was before Baptism, but the body of the regenerate becomes the flesh of the Crucified.

This, dearly beloved, is "the change from the right hand of the Highest," "who worketh all in all" (1 Cor 12:6), so that in the case of every faithful man we may, through the character of a good life, understand Him to be the author of pious works: giving thanks to the mercy of God, who so adorns the whole body of the Church by innumerable bestowals of spiritual gifts, that by the many rays of one light the same splendor is everywhere manifest, nor can the good desert Of any Christian be aught else than the glory of Christ.

This is that "true light which" justifies and "enlightens every man" (John 1:9). This is that which "rescues us from the power of darkness, and translates us into the kingdom of the Son of God" (Col 1:13). This is that which through newness of life elevates the desires of the soul, and quenches the appetites of the flesh. This is that whereby the Lord's Passover is legitimately celebrated "in the unleavened bread of sincerity and truth" (1 Cor 5:8); while, after the leaven of the old malice has been cast away, the new creature is exhilarated and fed from the Lord Himself. For the participation of the Body and Blood of Christ effects nothing else than this, that we pass into That which we receive; and as we have died with Him, and been buried with Him, and raised up with Him, so we bear Him throughout, both in spirit and in flesh, as the Apostle says: "For ye are dead, and your life is hid with Christ in God. For when Christ, your life, shall appear, then shall ye also appear with Him in glory" (Col 3:3-4).

15

CHRIST'S SOVEREIGNTY OVER ALL FLESH

THERE IS IN CHRISTIAN FAITH A VAST REGION OF SUPER-natural realities loudly proclaiming Christ's supreme victory. In strict theological language those realities are called the sacramental graces. They are, by their very nature, of such supremacy that unless we believe in the unrestricted mastery of Christ over all flesh we could hardly conceive that such things are possible. Through the sacraments Christ sanctifies the human race by the sheer domination of His supernatural empire.

It would take us too far if we were to expound here the sacramental doctrine of the Church in its entirety, though, for anyone who is writing on the victory of Christ, the temptation to do so is very great, for, from the first to the last, sacramental grace shows an independence of human conditions which is only possible in the hypothesis that the Son of God Himself has triumphed over all obstacles. Through water, through the laying on of hands, through bread and wine, through words and signs, the Son of God sanctifies the world with irresistible power, asking no more of man than that he should believe and repent. What in technical theology is called the *opus operatum*, "work worked," of the sacrament may well be described in terms of divine victory; but the whole sacramental life of the Church, in all its aspects, presupposes that an immense wealth of spiritual powers are always ready, knowing no obstacles, asking for leave from no man.

When Christ, for the first time, as far as we know, introduces the subject of the future sacraments, He silences the objections of Nicodemus who could not see how a man, being old, could be born again of water and the Holy Ghost. Christ's reply is merely a statement of the immensity of the activities of the Spirit:

> That which is born of the flesh is flesh: and that which is born of the Spirit is spirit. Wonder not that I said to thee: You must be born again. The Spirit breatheth where he will and thou hearest his voice: but thou knowest not whence he cometh and whither he goeth. So is every one that is born of the Spirit (John 3:6-8).

In order to make our meaning clearer we may take baptism as a perfect instance of this transcending sovereignty of Christ over all human beings. Water becomes an irresistible agent of sanctification under the breath of the victorious King, nothing can resist the power of baptismal water.

It is worth reflecting on the mode of speech which the early Church uses with regard to this element, water. When the hearts of the people were touched by the words of Peter in the hour when the Spirit was sent forth, they appealed to him and the other Apostles: "Men and brethren, what shall we do?" The reply is marvelously direct:

> Peter said to them: Do penance: and be baptized every one of you in the name of Jesus Christ for the remission of your sins. And you shall receive the gift of the Holy Ghost (Acts 2:38).

There is no hesitation, there is no groping about; there is no uncertainty: "be baptized every one of you in the name of Jesus Christ." An external rite, the simplest rite in the world, will bring them into immediate contact with the great spiritual power that is seen and heard by everybody, the Paraclete: "And you shall receive the gift of the Holy Ghost."

When the eunuch had been instructed by Philip on the road from Jerusalem to Gaza they came to a certain water; in this the man from Ethiopia sees his chance: "And the eunuch said: See here is water, what doth hinder me from being baptized?" Philip, the deacon, has only one condition; "If thou believest with all thy heart, thou mayest." The eunuch makes a profession of faith that is as simple as it is comprehensive: "I believe that Jesus Christ is the Son of God" (Acts 8:36, 37). The scene that follows is matchless in its unquestioning acceptance of Christ's power to sanctify anywhere and everywhere:

> And he commanded the chariot to stand still. And they went down into the water, both Philip and the eunuch. And he baptized him (Acts 8:38).

Again, Peter, after instructing the house of Cornelius, seeing how the Holy Spirit had come down on these catechumens, makes this remark, which to him was obvious:

> Can any man forbid water, that these should not be baptized, who have received the Holy Ghost, as well as we (Acts 10:47)?

The water of baptism, then, is spoken of by the early Church as being a divine power; water came from the pierced breast of Christ when He succumbed in the great battle, and from His death there sprang forth the river of life, baptism. We know how, in a way, every human being can baptize validly. Any soul crying out for the water, in any part of the world, is saved through that water. The doctrine of Christian baptism is such a stupendous assertion of Christ's power of sanctification that unless we hold fast to our faith in His universal conquest of mankind we could hardly bring ourselves to admit so universal a means of giving eternal life; for through this water countless millions of children are sanctified and are made heirs of the kingdom of heaven; through this water all sins are washed away, and the greatest criminal finds himself clothed in the white robes of the sons of the kingdom. It is not the act of man, it is the act of Christ. Faith and repentance is the one disposition which is presupposed in the adult, to make him the fit subject of this great regeneration.

Many more things we could say about the irresistible power of baptism, of its effects, even in spite of the sins of man and the unworthiness of the ministers, for it is truly Christ that baptizes through the human ministry, and the baptism of Christ is supremely efficacious because the dominion of Satan over mankind has been broken by Him.

Infant baptism is certainly one of our most marvellous articles of belief. To admit, as we do, that the new-born child can be given, at the very first moment of its existence, a second life incomprehensibly more lasting than the life it has from the mother's womb, is indeed to think in values which are entirely different from ordinary human standards. The child is as remote from a conscious rational act as could be possibly imagined; its physical life is of the frailest, and yet we say that its soul is in bondage to a dark power at one moment, through original sin, only to be translated into the kingdom of the Prince of Light by the sacrament of water. From that moment heaven is in the soul of that child and the breast of that little one is the temple of the Holy Ghost; if the feeble natural life should cease, if the child should die, one more spirit has gone to swell the ranks of the angels that stand before the Throne of God. Well might we ask with Nicodemus: "How can these things be?" The reply is, as always, "the victory of the Son of God."

We have already alluded to the intimate connection between Christ's resurrection and the power of remitting sin. The sacrament of penance is indeed another aspect of Christ's triumph; sin is remitted because sin has been overcome by Him. The power that effaces sin committed after baptism, is called the "power of the Keys"; this metaphor primarily represents the Apostolic jurisdiction vested in St. Peter and his brethren, but Christ Himself, as a result of His victory also holds the keys of life and death, of sin and grace:

> And to the angel of the church of Philadelphia write: These things saith the Holy One and the true one, he that hath the key of David, he that openeth and no man shutteth, shutteth and no man openeth (Rev 3:7).

The remission of sins which Christ entrusted to the Apostles on the first Easter day is essentially destined for the believer, for him who is baptized in Christ; for the triumph of the Son of God is not only this, that He should conquer man, bringing him out of infidelity and making him His own through baptism, but also His unlimited jurisdiction over His own and over their acts, so that He can forgive their sins without being obliged to give an account of His mercies. He is simply supreme in this matter of forgiveness because in His own Body He has destroyed all sin. The apparent facility with which the remission of sin is obtained by the faithful through the sacrament of penance is a scandal to many, but to all those who have true understanding of the victory of Christ the unceasing murmurings of the words of absolution in the confessionals all over the world are like the music of the heavenly *cortège* that follows the triumphant Christ.

It is chiefly through that entirely new form of supernatural life, the sacramental graces, that the Christian people have become the worthy recipients of an encomium like the one from the pen of St. Peter:

> But you are a chosen generation, a kingly priesthood, a holy nation, a purchased people; that you may declare his virtues, who hath called you out of darkness into his marvellous light (1 Pet 2:9).

Through the sacramental life in all its aspects the Christian people cry forth to the whole world the virtues of the divine Victor, who has made the kingdom of light to succeed the kingdom of darkness.

Of the Eucharist, as the sacrament of Christ's victory *par excellence*, we will speak in another chapter; in it there is the sacrificial aspect which constitutes an entirely new way for Christ's triumph to be brought home to man.

The Christian priesthood with its powers and *charismata*, is the army of a triumphant cause. The certainties of the Catholic sacerdotal ministry cannot be understood, in fact they would be hardly tolerable, if the priesthood did not speak in the Name of One whose Name is above all other names.

The Catholic contention that every marriage of Christians is a sacrament, again presupposes infinitely more than the world is ready to accept. It takes for granted that Christ's overlordship is not only an ideal of the mind, but that it is a juridical power which annuls every human undertaking that is against Christ's rights. The sanctification, moreover, of human propagation through a sacrament is not thinkable except through the assumption that the Son of God has power over all flesh, down to the very sources of human life.

In death we expect Christ to show forth His victory over the world, over sin, over Satan, in a most personal way in favor of each one of us. There is simply no end to the trust of the dying Christian. It is taken absolutely for granted that there can be no sort of peril or unknown evil awaiting the Christian soul on the other side, because the Son of God has overcome it all. There can be no rift in the armor of the Christian. If the chances of our encountering unforeseen dangers on our entering eternity were not more than one in a million, even that fraction would be big enough to take the laurels from Christ's forehead. He would not be the complete Victor. But our trust in Him cannot envisage even such a remote possibility of danger. The profession of that trust is couched in terms of undying splendor by St. Paul:

> Nor height, nor depth, nor any other creature, shall be able to separate us from the love of God which is in Christ Jesus our Lord (Rom 13:39).

16

CHRIST'S VICTORY AND THE CHURCH'S PERSECUTIONS

ONE OF THE PROFOUNDEST ORIGINALITIES OF CHRISTIANITY is in this, that its divine Founder makes it a part of His message to announce every kind of hardship and contradiction as the normal condition of existence for His followers. Were it not for the optimism that makes Him to declare all evil to be the road to victory Christ might be called a prophet of evil, for none has spoken more darkly of the future. His coming as the Redeemer of mankind does not mean the holding up of the human tragedy, of the ills that are the unavoidable accompaniment of the journey of the race:

> Nation shall rise against nation, and kingdom against kingdom. And there shall be great earthquakes in diverse places and pestilences and famines and terrors from heaven: and there shall be great signs (Luke 21:10-11).

Wars there will be, as much as and even more than ever. The *pressura gentium*, the "distress of nations," seems particularly the fate reserved to mankind in the days that follow the redemption by the God-Man.

Of the Golden Age there is not the faintest vestige in Christ's thought and speech. From the multitude of calamities Christ does not promise to His disciples physical immunity, though He constantly promises another immunity of a much higher kind. But there is even more than the announcement that the world would be left to its own sad destinies. Tribulations of a peculiar kind are in store for His disciples, and for His Church, precisely because they are His own:

> If the world hate you, know ye that it hath hated me before you. If you had been of the world, the world would love its own: but because you are not of the world, but I have chosen you out of the world, therefore the world hateth you. Remember my word that I said to you: The servant is not greater than his master. If they have persecuted me, they will also persecute you. If they have kept my word, they will keep yours also. But all these things they will do to you for my name's sake: because they know not him that sent me (John 15:18-21).

Christians will share in the identical misfortune which was Christ's own, namely to be put to death because men think they are doing a service to God by the very act. Jesus was crucified because the Jewish priesthood declared Him to be a blasphemer of God. So to His disciples Jesus says:

> These things have I spoken to you, that you may not be scandalized. They will put you out of the synagogues: yea, the hour cometh, that whosoever killeth you will think that he doth a service to God. And these things will they do to you; because they have not known the Father nor me (John 6:1-3).

Our Lord speaks of the great catastrophes and the persecutions and scandals as of things that are unavoidable: "For these things must come to pass" (Matt 24:6). Into a world thus doomed Christ sends His dear disciples, as "sheep among wolves." A more telling metaphor human imagination could not invent in order to describe the unfavorable milieu which this world is for the believer. So we are absolutely certain of this fact, that Christ's victory could not mean a providential alteration of the course of human destinies. This the Son of God never contemplated as belonging to His mission here on earth. His victory is inside those conditions, within the unfavourable milieu, "in the midst of His enemies," *in media inimicorum suorum.*

This, of course, is applicable only to the present aeon, to the time that is now. In reality, Christ's victory over adverse circumstances is as complete as His triumph over sin and death. For the endless ages of eternity the absolute sovereignty of Christ will be as manifest as all His other attributes. No head will be raised up against Him. In comparison with eternity the time of trial, measured as duration, is as nothing. Compared with the infinitude of the glorious eternity, thousands of years of Church history, with all their narratives of persecution, are in reality not much longer than the thirty-three years of Christ's mortal life, when He was in the state of *kenosis*, of humiliation.

But if in true reckoning the days are few, they are certainly evil, very evil, and their darkness might obscure for us the supreme fact that Christ is truly victorious. But with His frankness in announcing the evils to come Christ unites invariable solemn assurances that nothing can hurt us. He seems to take a delight in this contrast, the mountainous form of the evils and their complete powerlessness to do His disciples any harm: "But a hair of your head shall not perish" (Luke 21:18).

It is not only the general watchfulness of God's providence, it is a direct dispensation that is the cause of this preservation in the midst of cataclysms; the immunity of the elect is part of Christ's own immunity from evil. For though Christ conquered Satan, sin and death, He succumbed externally to the ferocity of His enemies. So the elect may succumb, but they cannot be hurt in their real life. Above all, the transient success of the powers of darkness is unable to produce in them the impression that Christ's cause is weak; for they see with a clear vision the coming of judgement. They are not seduced, they are not led to alter their faith in Christ, to think of Him otherwise than in terms of immutable majesty.

> Then if any man shall say to you, Lo, here is Christ, or there: do not believe him. For there shall arise false Christs and false prophets and shall show great signs and wonders, insomuch as to deceive (if possible) even the elect (Matt 24:23-24).

This is the supreme grace and genius of Christianity: that the signs and wonders of false prophets cannot seduce the minds of the faithful.

What Christ had said repeatedly concerning the Christian's immunity from real harm in a world full of woes, has been magnificently amplified by that Spirit who was sent to announce the things that are to come:

> For he shall not speak of himself: but what things soever he shall hear, he shall speak. And the things that are to come he shall show you (John 16:13).

These words of Christ make it evident that some "showing" of future events is part of the Spirit's mission. This was done chiefly through the Revelation of St. John called the Apocalypse:

> And the Lord God of the spirits of the prophets sent his angel to show his servant the things which must be done shortly (Rev 22:6).

The great prophecy of John, the beloved disciple, is a fit conclusion to the Scriptures, not only through the splendor of the vision, but chiefly through the greatness of the lesson it inculcates, the persistence of the Lamb's triumph in spite of every adversity and every hostility. In the Apocalypse, as in the Gospels, the external condition under which the elect live is put before us with merciless frankness. There are dark passages like this:

> And it was given unto him (the dragon) to make war with the saints and to overcome them. And power was given to him over every tribe and people and tongue (Rev 13:7).

Yet with all those concessions to the powers of darkness the real issue is never doubtful; the evil powers will fight the Lamb with one accord, but it is all in vain:

> These shall fight with the Lamb. And the Lamb shall overcome them, because he is the Lord of lords and King of kings: and they that are with him are called and elect and faithful (Rev 17:4).

We may, in a way, readily understand why the revelation of God to man should be crowned with a prophetic vision of the future; it will always be the Christian's chief practical difficulty to see a victorious Christ through the overshadowing clouds of human events. More than once the words of the Apocalypse will be fulfilled, "And the sun became black as sackcloth of hair: and the whole moon became as blood" (Rev 6:12), but at no time is the actual figure of the divine fighter obscured; He rides forth as an invincible conqueror.

It is a striking feature of that wonderful book that no clear distinction is drawn in it between the final triumph of Christ at the end of all times and the triumph of Christ in the present aeon. Many of the glorious scenes of victory depicted in the Apocalypse are applicable and have to be applied to both states, the final, eschatological state and the present, transient state of temptation. It would be distinctly wrong not to apply to our present conditions some of the tableaux of victory delineated by the great seer. It is the spirit of St. John, we might even say the genius of St. John, in all his writings, in his Gospel, in his Epistles, in his Revelation to show how the mystery of the eternal life, the mystery of the divine victory, is of the present time as well as of the future world; how the eternal life is in us now, how we have the victory over the world now, though the full meaning of that life and of that victory will be revealed then only when Christ shall appear in glory.

There is no reason why we should not apply to the Christian people of the present time that description which constitutes one of the most famous passages in the Apocalypse though, by a natural transition, the image moves from the present aeon into the state of eternity. We could not conclude this chapter more usefully than by quoting it here, exhorting our readers to think of themselves as being members of that wonderful people. One of the arguments adduced in order to prove that St. John speaks of earthly conditions, at least to begin with, is this: the multitude which he sees is "of all nations and tribes and peoples and tongues" (Rev 7:9); this formula naturally points to earthly conditions.

And after this, I saw a great multitude, which no man could number, of all nations and tribes and peoples and tongues, standing before the throne and in sight of the Lamb, clothed with white robes, and palms in their hands. And they cried with a loud voice, saying: Salvation to our God, who sitteth upon the throne, and to the Lamb. And all the angels stood round about the throne and the ancients and the four living creatures. And they fell down before the throne upon their faces and adored God, saying: Amen. Benediction and glory and wisdom and thanksgiving, honor and power and strength, to our God for ever and ever. Amen.

And one of the ancients answered and said to me: These that are clothed in white robes, who are they? And whence came they? And I said to him: My Lord, thou knowest. And he said to me: These are they who are come out of great tribulation and have washed their robes and have made them white in the blood of the Lamb. Therefore, they are before the throne of God; and they serve him day and night in his temple. And he that sitteth on the throne shall dwell over them. They shall no more hunger nor thirst: neither shall the sun fall on them, nor any heat. For the Lamb, which is in the midst of the throne, shall rule them and shall lead them to the fountains of the waters of life: and God shall wipe away all tears from their eyes (Rev 7:9-17).

It is the present-day Christian who can be said to be standing before the throne and in the sight of the Lamb, clothed with a white robe and with a palm in his hand, because through his faith and his grace he is truly in the midst of the divine mystery.

17

The Eucharist,
The Monument of Christ's Victory

W<small>E MUST TAKE IT AS A FUNDAMENTAL PRINCIPLE OF</small> Christian thought that the Christ who presides over the destinies of the Church is the victorious, the triumphant Christ, and the One who said, "Behold I am with you every day until the end of times" (Matt 28:20), is the conqueror of Satan, sin, and death. So all the manifestations of Christ's power and presence are, by their very nature, exhibitions of the divine victory.

Even when we celebrate the memories of Christ's Passion and Death, we are perpetually and invariably conscious of the glories that followed after. So we are justified in looking upon every one of the sacraments of the Church as a direct act of divine conquest of the human race by the Christ who dwells in glory. Through the sacraments, from the Right Hand of God, Jesus enters into the very flesh and bone of the human race as an assimilating power, binding man to Himself, on the whole irresistibly.

But there is one sacrament which truly may be called the sacrament of Christ's victory because through its very constitution it is

a quasi-monument here on earth of the great achievement of the
Son of God, the liberation from all evils through His Blood. This
sacrament is the blessed Eucharist. In it we celebrate Christ's triumph with a directness of purpose that leaves nothing to be desired
as to the true significance of that venerable sacrament. It is difficult
to find terms for realities so uncommon and so new to human
experience.

One would fain ask leave to coin expressions that would in a
way do justice to one's thinking, if not to the reality itself, for one
must take it for granted that no human language could ever do
justice to that. So I should like to speak of the mystery of Christ's
victory as the mystery of "immortal death," *mors immortalis*, and
this for two reasons. Firstly, the death of Christ is an event which,
historically speaking, happened once, but which, in the dispensation of the Christian sacrament of the Eucharist, is perpetuated in a
mystical way. Then, secondly, I call Christ's death immortal because
immortality was so much a part of that passing away of Christ on
the Cross that the death of Jesus must be truly considered as a short
and miraculous interruption of His native immortality.

This immortality surrounds the death of Jesus as the waters
of the ocean press from all sides on the deep keel of a ship, urged
by their native mobility to fill up the gap as the keel moves on.
Not mortality but immortality was Christ's natural condition
even whilst here on earth; so His death could never be regarded
as an event in itself, but must be read in the light of the vaster
event, the rapidly-returning immortality, in other words, the resurrection.

Perhaps my reader will be helped at this juncture by a fuller explanation of the statement just made that Christ's condition here below

was one of immortality, not of mortality. As such an explanation is calculated to be helpful to the main idea of this chapter, I tarry willingly a moment, in order to give it. Nothing could happen to Christ that would necessarily end His life here on earth; He laid it down Himself; the divinity that was in Him could always prevent the separation between soul and body which, in human language, is death. He Himself committed His soul to His Father. So we have to admit that if cruelties that would mean death for ordinary mortals were done to Christ's human nature, in His case death would not follow unless He willed it, for as a divine Person he had full possession of that soul which would not leave the body except by His will. Says St. Thomas:

> Christ's spirit had the power to keep the nature of His flesh, so that it would not be crushed by any hurt whatsoever inflicted on it. This power the soul of Christ possessed because it was united with the word of God in oneness of Person, as Augustine says in the fourth book on the Trinity. As Christ, then, of His own accord, did not repulse from His own body the hurt done to it, but willed that His bodily nature should succumb to the injury, it is truly said that He laid down His soul or that He died of His own accord (III, q. 47, a. 1).

St. Leo abounds in this sense:

> Although the ferocity of the Jews was aflame and ready to carry out their criminal design, yet no violence could have been done to the temple of Christ's body had He not allowed it Himself, because God was in Christ, reconciling the world unto Himself. But as it was determined that another kind of work (than

an effect of the divine omnipotence) should bring about the liberation of mankind, and as otherwise the Blood of Christ could not have been the price of the redemption of the believers, had the Savior not been laid hold upon, He allowed the godless to stretch forth their hand against Him. He kept in check the power of the Godhead, so that the glory of the Passion might be reached, *Cohabita est potentia Deitatis ut perveniretur ad gloriam Passionis* (St. Leo, Sermon 65).

St. Thomas in the passage quoted above refers us to St. Augustine. The Bishop of Hippo speaks in the language of the Pope of Rome, so we read in the Fourth Book *de Trinitate*, "On the Trinity":

The Mediator did not leave His flesh against His will, but because He willed, when He willed and as He willed, because He was united to the word of God in oneness of Person. ... It is not because some power had jurisdiction over Him that He was deprived of His bodily life, but He Himself stripped Himself of it: for He who had it in His power not to die if He did not want to die, without any doubt died because He so willed, and therefore He held in mockery principalities and powers, showing unhesitatingly His victory over them in His own Person. For this was His purpose in dying, that through the one most true Sacrifice (*uno verissimo sacrificio*) offered up for us, He might cleanse and abolish and extinguish whatever claim there was through our sins for the principalities and powers to make us the objects of just punishment (St. Augustine, *De Trinitate*, 4.13).

We see here how St. Augustine, by a natural sequence of thought, identifies the two concepts, sacrifice and voluntary death.

Coming then to the great memory of the Lord, the divine Eucharist, it is as much the sacrament of Christ's resurrection as of Christ's death, because it is the memory or monument of that death like unto which there is no death. It is a commemoration of that victorious passage unto the Father, that new and supreme Passover, of which the first Passover was a faint figure. Therefore as often as we eat that Bread and drink of that Cup we show forth the death of the Lord until He come, a death that is in every respect a triumph, because the "coming" here alluded to is not a coming from the realm of the dead, from Hades, but from the kingdom of eternal life.

The phrase of St. Paul, "until He come," how easily it could have been twisted into a half-pagan meaning, into the expectation of the return of a dead hero! But Christian sentiment has been proof against any such distortion. The dead Lord's coming that is part of the Eucharistic significance, the Eucharistic showing forth, is a coming out of the realms of glory and life. The world has never known a rite of such triumphant signification, wherein the whole meaning is a victory of unsurpassed proportion. The Real Presence lifts that rite into the region of the infinite and the absolutely divine. Nothing in the Eucharist speaks of failure or loss; everything proclaims fulfillment of the desires of the Son of God:

> And when the hour was come, he sat down: and the twelve apostles with him. And he said to them: with desire I have desired to eat this pasch with you, before I suffer. For I say to you that from this time I will not eat it, till it be fulfilled in the kingdom of God (Luke 22:14-16).

Christ from the supper-room sees the glorious future, the Eucharist that is food and drink in the kingdom of God, the

Christian Church.

So the sacrament of the Body and the Blood is above all things a thanksgiving, a *Eucharistia*, for the great victory. As a thanksgiving for victory its prototype appears for the first time when Melchizedech the high priest offers bread and wine:

> But Melchizedech, the king of Salem, bringing forth bread and wine, for he was the priest of the Most High God, blessed him and said: Blessed be Abram by the Most High God, who created heaven and earth. And blessed be the Most High God, by whose protection the enemies are in thy hands. And he gave him the tithes of all (Gen 14:18-20).

The Eucharist is the sacrifice of thanksgiving for the victory of Christ in all its manifold aspects. As it is a commemoration, the element of thanksgiving must, as a matter of course, be predominant; for the event, the liberation of captive humanity through the death of Christ, could not be remembered except with supreme gratitude. In the words of the sacred Council of Trent, the Eucharist is a pasch, a feast of rejoicing, for ever commemorating the passing from servitude unto liberty:

> Christ instituted a new pasch, when He gave Himself to be immolated by the Church through the hands of the priests under visible signs, in memory of that passage of His from this world unto the Father, when He redeemed us through the pouring forth of His Blood, when He delivered us from the power of darkness and brought us into His own Kingdom (*Council of Trent*, Session 22, chap. 1).

It is Catholic faith that the Eucharistic sacrifice is "one and the same with the sacrifice" of the Cross: *una enim et eadem est hostia.* There is this, however—and through this circumstance the identity of the sacrifice is not interfered with—the Eucharistic sacrifice is the *memoria,* the commemoration, of the sacrifice of the Cross, and therefore its thanksgiving, its song of praise and victory.

We might be permitted to say that the death of the Lord, the remembrance of which is the very essence of the sacrifice of the Christian altar, appears in the Eucharist chiefly from that aspect of immortality which we said belongs to it at all times. So in the same breath the Church commemorates at Mass Christ's death, resurrection and ascension, as belonging to the great remembrance, because, truly, Christ's death was always and necessarily a passing from this world unto the Father, unto glory and majesty. Christ's death is different in this from all other deaths. And so the Eucharist, though essentially a memory of the dying of Christ, is quite naturally a triumphant act of Christ, performed on the altars of Christendom.

One of the technical modes of stating the Eucharistic sacrifice is that the Mass is said to apply to us all the fruits of the sacrifice of the Cross; this is simply another way of declaring the same mystery. It is the triumph, the dividing of the spoils after the successful battle.

The Eucharistic sacrifice is in no way prejudicial to the redemptive efficacy of the sacrifice of the Cross, as the Council of Trent again is careful to remind us. It is not a new merit added to the merits of Christ's cruel death on Calvary. It is essentially a triumph, a celebration of the act done before, the victory of the bloody struggle of the first Good Friday. No hymn of rejoicing is too enthusiastic, no manifestation of joy is excessive in those who are privileged to be the sacrificants of the Christian altar. The hymn of the medieval theologian has said it so well:

Quantum potes, tantum aude:
Quia major omni laude
  Nec laudare sufficis.

Strive thy best to praise Him well,
Yet doth He all praise excel;
  None can ever reach His due;

Even when we celebrate Mass in a penitential spirit, for the remission of our sins, the note of victory is not less clear, because we are reconciled to God in virtue of the showing forth of the divine Blood under the sacramental veil, as it is the glory of the risen life. In this sense the Eucharist is truly a heavenly sacrifice because its two adorable elements, the Body and the Blood, are not of earth but of heaven. So Christian tradition has it that the hosts of heaven surround the altar on which the divine mysteries are celebrated.

The Council of Trent gives us another hint that makes us perceive, at least dimly, another aspect of that invincibility of glory which belongs to the Eucharist. The Council says that "this immaculate sacrifice cannot suffer any stain through the iniquity of man," *Et haec quidem illa munda oblatio est, quae nulla indignitate aut malitia offerentium inquinari potest* (*Council of Trent*, Session 22, chap. 1). In other words, the Eucharistic sacrifice is independent of human worth; the unworthy priest cannot throw a shadow into that world of light which is the Eucharist; even when he offers Mass with a sin-stained conscience, the faith of the Church, who is the real sacrificant, transcends the individual shortcomings of her minister. So the priest in the Canon prays that God look not at his sins but at the faith of the Church, *Ne respicias peccata mea sed fidem Ecclesiae tuae.*

The partaking of that sacrifice, Holy Communion, is essentially and intrinsically in the nature of a banquet; it is eating the Flesh and drinking the Blood that gave life to the world; it is a participation in the Cup of the Lord, it is an eating at the table of the Lord, in opposition to the dark and sinister rites of paganism that were an enslavement to Satan:

> You cannot drink the chalice of the Lord and the chalice of devils; you cannot be partakers of the table of the Lord and of the table of devils (1 Cor 10:21).

Festiveness is the only temper which Christians may bring to the reception of that heavenly bread; they cannot be sad, they must rejoice with the angels in heaven when eating that divine manna. It is not known to the history of Christian spirituality that the faithful ever approached the Eucharistic table with other dispositions than those of gladness and triumph; at Holy Communion Christians join the white-robed army which stands before the throne of God and of the Lamb. To be allowed to partake of the altar, of the offering that is on the altar, is the supreme privilege of religion; it makes the distinction between the adherent of that religion and the outsider, or even the mere aspirant:

> We have an altar whereof they have no power to eat who serve the tabernacle (Heb 13:10).

The servers of the Jewish tabernacle are excluded from participation at the Christian altar: such exclusion is the severest and most persistent law of the Church. The faithful, on the contrary, have the privilege of that participation of the altar. This participation, in the words of one of the oldest and most mysterious prayers of the Canon of the Mass, gives to them the sacrosanct Body and Blood of Christ with all heavenly benediction and grace:

> We beseech Thee, O Lord God Almighty ... that all those of us who shall have taken the sacrosanct Body and Blood of Thy Son in virtue of this our participation of the altar (*ex hac altaris participatione*), may be filled with every kind of heavenly blessing and grace.

The words *ex hac altaris participatione* are one of the profoundest liturgical terms, difficult of translation, because they express an idea from which we have been estranged to a large extent, namely, that Holy Communion is essentially a participation of the altar.

18

THE BEHAVIOR OF THE BELIEVER
IN CHRIST'S VICTORY

TOTALITY OF ATONEMENT FOR HUMAN SIN THROUGH Christ is a faith so vast and so astonishing that, in a way, all merely human calculations in the ethical order are upset by it. What becomes of human guilt in the face of a justice so overwhelming and so unlimited as is the justice of the atoning Son of God, who was made sin for us that through Him we should become justice? So there is every reason for us to ask the question, how do men who sincerely believe in atonement—in other words, in the victory of Christ—view human sin? Ought we not to expect them to make light of human sin for this very reason, that in Christ Jesus it is made dead, it is as if it had not been a life action on the part of man?

For let us always remember the atonement is a destruction of sin, according to the energetic language of St. Paul. We can never say enough concerning the power of the Blood of Christ to do away with sin; it pursues sin and destroys it with a kind of divine fury. What then is left of sin? Has it any horror, any sting after the passing of the

Blood of the Lamb? Is not every sin committed by men in the course of the ages in a way still-born, since the Lamb of God, long ago, has taken upon Himself all the sins of the world and destroyed them in His own Body on the tree of the Cross?

We ought not to marvel if the minds of believers have been dazzled at times by the victory of the Cross, and have not found it easy to state clearly the respective places of the two opposite powers, the power of sin and the power of the atonement. But it may be asserted without fear of contradiction that universal Christian sentiment has been, and is, a real and sincere horror of sin, a horror that is all the greater because Christ died to wipe away all iniquity. Sin, in popular language, has crucified Christ, and that very death of God which destroys sin makes the full hideousness of that sin appear before the eyes of all men.

We may not be able to find a key to this psychological state of the Christian conscience, but the fact is indubitable: faith in the Atonement has not diminished dread of sin in practical life amongst Christians, but has enormously increased it. But no doubt the theological explanation is not beyond our reach. Christ has hated sin; this is the reason of His readiness to shed His blood as a cleansing of sin. Through His Spirit the Son of God instills into the heart of Christians the very feelings that are in Himself; His own heart's horror at the aspect of sin is to be found in the heart of those that are His. The Christian fear of sin is, of course, essentially supernatural, that is to say, it is caused by the Holy Ghost: in other words, it is a participation in Christ's own detestation of every offence against God. This detestation was the cause of His profound humiliation, of His ignominious death on the Cross. So there can be no other attitude for the Christian towards sin than a similar detestation, with the bitter remembrance that the Son of God was thus degraded through bearing our sin:

> For let this mind be in you, which was also in Christ Jesus: who, being in the form of God, thought it not robbery to be equal with God: but emptied himself, taking the form of a servant, being made in the likeness of men, and in habit found as a man. He humbled himself, becoming obedient unto death, even to the death of the cross (Phil 2:5-8).

The destruction of sin which Christ undertook, if fully comprehended, includes this, that through His Spirit He should produce in His followers a detestation, similar to His own, of all iniquity.

If, having been told that God has atoned for all sin, man were left to appraise its meaning by his sole natural resources, he might indeed be very uncertain how to do so; but such is by no means the Christian hypothesis. Man is given, direct, a share in Christ's own Spirit, that Spirit of sanctity who prompted Him to offer Himself up as a pure oblation for all the defilement of the human race. The spirit of repentance for sin committed has thus become one of the main features of Christian spiritual life. It may truly be called the human side of the Atonement, man's own share in the mystery of the destruction of sin.

With our faith in Christ's victory over sin there is united our faith in the necessity of human repentance, so that there can be no question for the Christian of a falsifying of moral values and of a minimizing of ethical burdens on account of the basic fact of the divine act that makes sin appear as if it had not been. We must therefore look upon human contrition of heart for the voluntary trespasses of the will as the finite manifestation of the infinite mystery of the cleansing Blood of the Lamb. We do not, in Christian spirituality, repent isolatedly, but we repent in Christ, with some of the sorrow that filled His soul when He contemplated our infidelities towards God.

Faith in Christ's victory cannot lead to any kind of anomism, either in the speculative or practical order. By anomism is meant that special aberration of man which makes him believe that he is freed from all law because he holds a privileged place, because he is the object of some quite special favor. It would be anomism if anyone thought himself at liberty to act as he chooses because Christ has paid before for all delinquencies.

Now such an aberration could never be the consequence of an unquestioning acceptance of the fact that Christ has overcome all evil. Human repentance is part of that victory, as we have already said more fully when treating of the remission of sin through Christ's resurrection. It would be of little service here to go into the historical side of this matter, and examine whether or not such anomism has manifested itself, at least in a partial way, in the course of the life of the Church.

The name of Luther naturally comes to one's mind, as the originator of Protestantism is credited with precisely such a one-sided view of Christ's redemptive triumph that neither good works on the part of man, nor repentance has any place in his scheme of human salvation. We might say that Luther is the one instance where faith in the Atonement has had the effect dreaded all along, that of making human guilt appear as nothing in face of an atoning sanctity so overwhelming as is that of Christ. But to do Luther justice, his anomism was only partial; his mind was bewildered by the divine stroke that nailed all human guilt to the Cross and effaced it in the Blood of the divine Victim. But his belittling, on that account, of the necessity of human repentance was not wholehearted; it was full of compromises with the traditional Christian psychology, which, as we have seen, is a marvellous blending of God's act and man's sorrow over sin.

19

THE RELIGION OF VICTORY

THE BASIC FACT OF CHRIST'S VICTORY AFFECTS CHRISTIANITY in all its forms, whether it be private religion or official worship. The Christian must think of himself as of one who has been bought with a great price; he must think of the world as being redeemed; and he must view all the events of human history as being subsidiary to a fully-established and inflexible plan of spiritual liberation. It is therefore not too much to say that Christian religion differs not only in degree but in kind from natural religion. Owing to this presupposition of a consummated state of spiritual conquest there is in Christian worship an element that is unique and quite original. We perform acts of adoration, of thanksgiving; we pray, we intercede, we crave for forgiveness, as other religious men who also have the faith of God have done and are doing; but we do more because the Divine has come much nearer to us through the mystery of the Incarnation and through the advent of the Holy Ghost.

It is, however, no longer a higher prayer, but a different prayer when we deal with God essentially as Christians, that is to say, in the Name of Christ and in the name of His victory. For this is the Christian's privilege, that he arrives before God and remains with God in virtue of the great conquest made by the Only Begotten Son of God. We may call this the dividing of the spoils amongst the followers of the divine Captain after the victorious battle. It ought to be evident, even to the least thoughtful, that the victory of Christ has brought into the supernatural world and into man's relationship with God, an entirely new element, quite unsuspected before. Man is not only a supplicant in the Face of his Maker, he is the partaker of a glorious condition of things; he is fellow heir with Christ; the good things that come to Christ through His mighty victory fall also into the laps of Christ's brethren. Any worship that left out of consideration this supreme addition to the supernatural order, would be not only imperfect but positively defective Catholicism.

However sincere and ardent adoration, praise, thanksgiving, might be, if Catholic worship had nothing more than these functions it would not be essentially higher than ancient Judaism. But it has something that is all its own and we may call it "the religion of victory." We Christians ought to feel as a nation feels when, with its king, it celebrates the day of victorious peace that ends a long war. The rejoicing of sovereign and people is a common rejoicing, the advantages of the successful contest are common advantages, the glory of it belongs to every member of the nation. This is only a feeble simile in order to express a mighty spiritual reality. Christian souls in their multitudes are fellow-victors with Christ; the day of Christ's triumphal ascending is their day of rejoicing, and the air of gladness is everywhere.

There is more than that: there is the partaking in the spoils. There is in Christian religion this one thing which, of course, no other religion ever professed to possess: there is the claim to definite advantages on the part of the faithful because Christ has conquered. Christian prayer may be intercession and supplication, but it may also be the statement of a claim; we lay our hands on definite goods and we call them our own, because we belong to the kingdom of the triumphant Christ:

> But to every one of us is given grace, according to the measure of the giving of Christ. Wherefore he saith: Ascending on high, he led captivity captive: he gave gifts to men. Now that he ascended, what is it, but because he also descended first into the lower parts of the earth? He that descended is the same also that ascended above all heavens; that he might fill all things (Eph 4:7-10).

This is the true meaning of prayer through Christ, a new prayer, not known before, because previous to that great victory no man dared to claim a share in the gifts of God. This is indeed the innermost meaning of Catholic liturgy. Liturgy is more than worship, it is worship plus that great claim of which we have spoken just now. If there were no justification for such a claim there would not be, properly speaking, a liturgy. When the Catholic approaches God, he approaches Him in the Name of Christ, in the name of Christ's merits, in the name of Christ's redemption, in one word: in the name of Christ's victory. The formula *per Dominum nostrum Jesum Christum*, "through our Lord Jesus Christ," acquires true meaning precisely through this claim which Christian faith inserts into religion, and which no religion ever possessed before:

> And in that day you shall not ask me anything. Amen, amen, I say to you: if you ask the Father anything in my name, he will give it you (John 16:23).

They do not ask, and yet it is granted; they ask in Christ's name, and it is granted. Could there be a clearer pronouncement concerning the Christian's right to possess the riches of the Son of God? Catholic liturgy, therefore, is more a celebration than a supplication; it speaks to God, it reminds God of all that has been achieved; it is a direct entering into the treasure house of God; it is a free partaking of the banquet of God. Unless we had this sense of spiritual possession which comes to us through Christ's conquest, we should have no true liturgy, we should have only the ordinary human prayer.

It is obvious, then, that the whole sacramental system, with the blessed Eucharist as its center, is an evident embodiment of this new relationship between God and man; what we have said in a preceding chapter on the victory of Christ through the sacraments and through the Eucharist is only another way of expressing the leading idea of this present chapter. The great theological notion of the *opus operatum* could be called the doctrine of man's claims on God, in virtue of Christ's conquest. Through the *opus operatum* we truly receive the best gifts and the most perfect gifts without asking for them. We receive them, not through supplication, but through celebration, through an official act which we perform with absolute certainty as God's ministers. With a firm step we enter into the Holy of Holies, carrying the prize of the divine victory, and there is the distribution of these gifts of the risen Christ on a scale truly divine.

It is, of course, to be expected that the denial of the sacramental theology of the Catholic Church would mean a complete reversal of conditions in man's intercourse with God; such a denial must of necessity be the end of what we call here the religion of victory. It is to be remarked, however, that interference with the sacramental doctrine of the Church on the part of Protestantism was not so radical as might have appeared at first sight. Under a disguise and under different names, some of the Reformers really clung to the doctrine of the *opus operatum*, of a distribution of divine favors beyond the merits of man's acts. No greater blow could be dealt to the Christian economy of grace than a refusal to admit divine largesses which are far in excess of man's merit, whether this be through the sacraments or through some other channel; it would reduce the position of the victorious Christ to that of a mere auxiliary of man instead of the Prince of Glory who enriches all those who follow Him.

Although the religion of victory shines with greatest brightness on the sacramental life, it would be wrong to think that the other acts of the supernatural life of the Christian are devoid of that quality; besides the divine claim, the Christian has the ordinary powers of prayer, of supplication, of intercession; but these powers in their turn, have been transformed and elevated through the fact of Christ's victory. The Christian prayer has a perfection all its own through this divine circumstance, that it is "through Jesus Christ." The Christian implores divine forgiveness whenever he has sinned, but his cry for mercy is not like the repentance of another man, because his prayer for forgiveness becomes part of a divine advocacy, of a static prayer that is more than intercession or supplication:

> My little children, these things I write to you that you may not sin. But if any man sin, we have an advocate with the Father, Jesus Christ the just. And he is the propitiation for our sins: and not for ours only, but also for those of the whole world (1 John 2:1-2).

Whatever is indispensable to the life of the soul, either as an individual or as a society, comes to us through a divine promise, through that settled estate which is called Christ's inheritance; the Father gives it to us because He loves us, and He loves us because we love the Son; we are expected to ask, but the asking is not the cry of the outcast, but a reminder that we are the sons of God and the lovers of Christ and as such we expect to be heard.

> Because I go to the Father: and whatsoever you shall ask the Father in my name, that will I do: that the Father may be glorified in the Son. If you shall ask me anything in my name, that will I do (John 14:13-14).

> If you abide in me and my words abide in you, you shall ask whatever you will: and it shall be done unto you (John 15:7).

If we call divine praise "liturgy" as we ought to do, then, of course, the identity between the religion of victory and liturgy is manifest. Our hymns to God and His Christ must be songs of victory, for we are like those who come home after having overcome the enemy and who have loaded themselves with spoils.

It may perhaps be urged as an objection against the idea of complete originality which we claim for Catholic liturgy that most of its wordings are the Psalms and Canticles of the Old Testament. Has Christianity really a worship different in kind, if the bulk of its liturgy is borrowed from the Jewish religion? Such an objection could only be made by those who are strangers to the Catholic doctrine of Scriptural inspiration. The Old Testament is the preparation for the New Dispensation; the Psalms and the Prophecies are full of Christ; Christ is in the Canticles of David and in the Canticles of Moses. He explains to the disciples, after the resurrection, all that those ancient hymns say of Him; it is a supreme evidence of His being the expected Messiah.

We are not surprised, therefore, that the Christian mysteries are celebrated and expressed with best results when we make use of the language of the Old Testament. The liturgical prayers and hymns which are the composition of the Church herself, I mean of her pontiffs, doctors, saints and poets, are one long canticle of victory. A slight change may, no doubt, be noticed in some of the modern compositions, where the note of sympathy for the offended Deity is more noticeable. But this nuance is so slight that it cannot make a difference to the universal song of praise that rises day and night to the throne of the victorious Christ.

To quote from the liturgical books of the Church would be superfluous, as every prayer might be cited in evidence of the Church's true spirit. One well-known canticle, however, may be alluded to, the *Exultet* of the Holy Saturday celebration. Its popularity is no reason for not referring to it with love:

Let the angelic choirs of heaven now rejoice; let the divine mystery rejoice; and let the trumpet of salvation resound for the victory of so great a king. Let the earth also rejoice, illumined with such splendor; and, enlightened by the brightness of the eternal king, let it feel that the darkness of the whole world is dispersed. Let also our Mother, the Church, rejoice, adorned with the brightness of so great light; and may this temple resound with the loud voices of the people.

20

THE VICTORY OF THE CHRISTIAN

IT IS ONE OF THE MOST PERMANENT FEATURES OF CHRISTIAN spiritual literature to describe the higher life in terms of victory. Not only the supreme fidelity of martyrdom is hailed as a victory, but every advance of man in the supernatural life is an overcoming, a defeating of an adverse power. In Christ Himself, this wide application of the metaphor of victory to all the phases and acts of the spiritual order would not be a correct reading of the facts. The Son of God made Man had no opposition to defeat, no darkness to overcome in His own interior life. He was sinless and infinitely above all the allurements of human temptations. He had the clear Vision and the perfect possession of God; so that it cannot be said of Him that He had the gifts of faith and hope, as He was already *in termino*, in that very center towards which other men are led gradually by faith and hope.

His internal charity was no struggle to Him as He was perfect in all things. His struggle, and therefore His victory, was in the external work which the Father had given Him to do, the work of redemption, as we have said in a previous chapter. In this, then, we differ from our Redeemer. The whole supernatural order without exception is not congenital to us as it is to Christ. It is grafted on a raw, desperately undivine nature, and we are strangers and foreigners to grace, to begin with. So it is true to say that the supernatural dispensation is not held by us except through a constant struggle, is not made use of by us except through an effort, and every step forward, every achievement in our spiritual life is truly a victory. Fidelity unto the end is described as such by the Spirit of Jesus:

> To him that shall overcome, I will give to sit with me in my throne: as I also have overcome and am set down with my Father in his throne. He that hath an ear, let him hear what the Spirit saith to the churches (Rev 3:21-22).

The grace of Christ in the souls He has conquered is not only abundant, it is multifarious. It has never escaped the masters of the life of the spirit that there is a variety of ways within the one great dispensation of Christian sanctity. For some centuries the distinction between the active and the contemplative way has been much stressed, perhaps unduly stressed; still the distinction has the advantage of bringing before our eyes the great fact of the variousness of the grace of Christ. But there is no grace, to whichever way it belongs, that is not a conquest of the soul by the spirit, a surrender of man's mind and will to a higher Power, nay, a victory within man's own intimate personality, one side of the human individuality rising superior to the other.

In this matter Catholic supernatural life parts company with the whole army of modern psychologists. Our higher life as Christians is essentially a state that does not belong to us; it is in every instance a conquest; it is the sovereignty of an external power, not the expression of our own self or the development of what is in us. This, of course, is evident in the whole sphere of the supernatural *per essentiam*, "essentially," in the supernatural, properly so-called; in faith, hope and charity, the workings of the sevenfold Spirit within us. In all these activities we are conquered by God, we are led into captivity by God, we are taken hold of in a most masterful way by God, we are no longer our own.

Faith is a power that, in the words of St. Paul, "bringeth into captivity every understanding into the obedience of Christ" (2 Cor 10:6). St. Thomas Aquinas, commenting on these words, says excellently, that in faith we submit to a stranger, to a truth that is not of our native soil, and therefore we are the prey of a victor, *Et inde est quod intellectus credentis dicitur esse captivatus quia tenetur terminis alienis* (*De Veritate*, q. 14, a. 1).

Hope is the brave deed to throw oneself forward into the unseen of God, against all experience.

Charity is the preference given to the one who is not ourselves before ourselves. It is always and everywhere victory, both active and passive; we are conquered by God and we conquer God.

St. Paul, for one, felt keenly the foreign origin of our whole supernatural life: "I live, but not I, but Christ liveth in me," *Vivo ego, iam non ego, vivit vero in me Christus* (Gal 1:20), is indeed his best known exclamation, revealing the constant atmosphere of his mind. Even when he breaks forth into enthusiastic praise of the new light that shines in the Christian's heart, he is all at once sobered by the thought that such a treasure is, after all, reposing in hearts that are very fragile receptacles:

For God, who commanded the light to shine out of darkness, hath shined in our hearts, to give the light of the knowledge of the glory of God, in the face of Christ Jesus. But we have this treasure in earthen vessels, that the excellency may be of the power of God and not of us. In all things we suffer tribulation: but are not distressed; we are straitened: but are not destitute (2 Cor 4:6-8).

Even those perfections of man which seem to belong to him with a more assured claim, his moral perfections, are still under the law of conquest as truly as the higher order. We cannot be the "square man," the homo quadratus, of the philosopher without an unceasing struggle:

Now then it is no more I that do it: but sin that dwelleth in me. For I know that there dwelleth not in me, that is to say, in my flesh, that which is good. For to will is present with me: but to accomplish that which is good, I find not. For the good which I will, I do not: but the evil which I will not, that I do (Rom 7:17-19).

The division in man is profound and permanent. There is unhappiness in us as there was in Paul: "Unhappy man that I am, who shall deliver me from the body of this death" (Rom 7:24)?

But there is no antagonism so violent between the flesh and the spirit, between the lower powers and the higher powers as not to be overcome by the grace of Christ. Christian asceticism is essentially optimistic; right through the ages there is the sound of the Canticle of the innumerable people who stand before the Lamb in white robes, with the palms of victory in their hands. From the hero of the ascetical golden age, the hermit of the early centuries, to our own more complicated civilization, there is the faith in man's power to be, through the grace of Christ, spotless and immaculate before God:

> He that shall overcome shall thus be clothed in white garments: and I will not blot out his name out of the book of life. And I will confess his name before my Father and before his angels (Rev 3:5).

The metaphor of the white garment is a New Testament metaphor, and its meaning is this: innocence through victory; the elect are in white garments because they overcame.

All we have said in this book concerning Christ's victory has a direct bearing on the individual life of man. We share in Christ's triumph now, here on earth, through that newness of life which comes to us from the resurrection:

> Now if we be dead with Christ, we believe that we shall live also together with Christ. Knowing that Christ, rising again from the dead, dieth now no more. Death shall no more have dominion over him. For in that he died to sin, he died once: but in that he liveth, he liveth unto God. So do you also reckon that you are dead to sin, but alive unto God, in Christ Jesus our Lord (Rom 6:8-11).

Just as there is no limit to Christ's sovereignty, so there is no limit to the possibilities of Christian sanctification, of the Christian's power to rise superior to all darkness and captivity of sin; we not only worship the victory of Christ but we are partakers in its virtue in our own mind, in our own members. This superiority of the Christian to all evils is, of course, a commonplace in New Testament thought; but though it be such a universal idea it is none the less marvellous and astonishing. The victory of Christ operates in us; His resurrection and His ascension are not only future hopes but actual, spiritual phenomena of our individual Christian life:

> God, Even when we were dead in sins, hath quickened us together in Christ (by whose grace you are saved). And hath raised us up together and hath made us sit together in the heavenly places, through Jesus Christ (Eph 2:5-6).

It is the merit of Catholic exegesis to read phrases like these not only in the light of the world to come, but in the light of the present times; our supernatural estate, as we possess it here on earth, is a resurrection and an ascension. Our conflicts with the external powers of darkness are, on the whole, only a small section of the great combat; few of us are destined to lay down our life for the Name of Christ, to share in Christ's testimony, to be martyrs; but we are all called to that high state of spiritual triumph, that mental illumination which it is so difficult to preserve in its untarnished brightness, the spontaneous and unquestioning acceptance of Christ's practical sovereignty over all flesh. So that we make our own the wonderful doxology of Jude the Apostle:

> Now to him who is able to preserve you without sin and to present you spotless before the presence of his glory with exceeding joy, in the coming our Lord Jesus Christ. To the only God, our Savior through Jesus Christ our Lord, be glory and magnificence, empire and power, before all ages, and now, and for all ages of ages. Amen (Jude 24-25).

EPILOGUE

I N TAKING LEAVE OF MY READER I MUST REMIND HIM ONCE
more of a truth which has been the undertone of all that has been
said in the preceding chapters, that a victorious Christ, such as I have
tried to describe, is the Church's supreme glory; Christians, in the
diversities of their graces, either individually or as a society, are victorious only in the victory of Christ.

I trust that no one will think me unkind in making here, at the
very end, when the reader is perhaps already exhausted, a statement
that may seem astonishing, but which is an original thought of our
master in divinity, St. Thomas Aquinas: "Christ," says the great doctor, "is the total wealth of the Church; He Himself, with the other
elect, is not greater than He Himself alone" (*Sent.* IV, d. 49, q. 4, a. 3,
ad 4). In other words, what is of utmost importance for the Church
is this, that her Christ should be what He is: He is the totality of her
goodness, the saints do not add to Him, but receive from Him. So
what really matters is our knowledge of what our Lord has achieved;
our achievements, big and small, are precontained in His mighty vic-

tory. No doubt many of us have to learn gradually this truly Christian method of appreciation; we must, of course, fall back on traditional theological principles. Modern sentiment is all for human achievements, and it looks at times as if man gave himself the air of a doer of things without any reference to Him who gives all the means necessary for the deed; even our Christian life and our spiritual career might suffer at times from this intellectual presumption unless we remember always that Christ has won our battles for us long before we were born.